ENGLISH NEEDLEWORK CARPETS

ENGLISH NEEDLEWORK CARPETS

16th to 19th Centuries

by

M. J. MAYORCAS

F.

TEXTILE BOOK SERVICE
266 LAKE AVE. • P. O. BOX 178
METUCHEN, NEW JERSEY 08840

PRINTED AND MADE IN ENGLAND

©
Copyright
F. Lewis, Publishers, Ltd.
The Tithe House
1461 London Road, Leigh-on-Sea
England

First published 1963

PRODUCED BY F. LEWIS, PUBLISHERS, LTD., AND PRINTED AT THE DOLPHIN PRESS LTD., BRIGHTON
BOUND BY LEIGHTON-STRAKER BOOKBINDING CO. LTD., LONDON

Contents

Preface

HITHERTO needlework carpets (woollen, linen or silk embroidery on canvas) have not merited more than a passing mention, or even perhaps an illustration or two in either carpet books, or books dealing with the art and history of needlecraft. It is because of this that I have endeavoured to produce a book of rare informative value and artistic quality for all who love the beauty and dignity of this almost forgotten craft.

Any useful craft, which has employed the energies and skills of innumerable earnest workers, cannot fail to be of interest. If the products of their industry have attained the highest degree of technical and artistic excellence, then there is a double claim on the attention of all those who can appreciate this unique combination of human art and craft.

It is doubtful whether any objects made by man or woman combine the qualities of beauty, durability (the examples illustrated are proof of this) and usefulness in such a high degree and such well-balanced proportions as needlework carpets. It may be surprising to many to learn that no book has been contributed before on English needlework carpets; such, however, is the case.

In order to try and fill this long overdue gap, I have attempted to collect, sift, check and re-check as many examples as possible. Only those considered to be worthy and artistic have been finally chosen. I am sure that this comprehensive collection, illustrated in chronological order, will, at the very least, help the reader to understand and love the history of this fascinating and much neglected art.

Most of the examples illustrated in this book, are known to me for one reason or another. Either because I have seen them in Museums, in collectors' houses, in houses open to the public, in public auctions, or finally in dealers' galleries.

Throughout this book, credits will be administered where due, to the many Museum Directors and Keepers of Textile Departments, who have been so kind in providing me with photographs and data, and to the many clients and friends, collectors and dealers, who have assisted me. My thanks to my dear wife Lilian, for her research on my behalf, and to my son, Mr. J. D. Mayorcas, for his very valuable help and information.

My special acknowledgments to A. F. Kendrick for his paper on *English Carpets* to The Royal Society of Arts 1919, to his *English Needlework* published 1933, to C. E. C. Tattersall's *History of British Carpets* 1934, whose chapter on Needlework Carpets I have pilloried. To the staff of the Reference Library of the Victoria and Albert Museum, for their courtesy, help and understanding. Finally my deepest thanks to Mr. Frank Lewis, for being so encouraging, helpful and patient, and for providing the incentive and opportunity of writing this book—a long cherished desire.

Introduction

A Brief History of Carpets in England

CARPETS[1] in the strict sense of a textile covering for the floor, were an unknown commodity in this country five hundred years ago. Until then, floors, if covered at all, were strewn with sweet rushes, hay, corn, foliage, fragrant herbs, or even flowers. These acted as a simple expedient to meet the most basic and crude human needs, principally, one presumes, with some hygienic motive. Obviously such simple coverings were easily and quickly replaceable, and a handy method of disposal was simply to eject them out of the nearest window! No consideration was exercised for the decorative or lasting aspects of floor-coverings as an integral part of furnishings.

This primitive attitude continued until the end of the 16th century, to the consternation of at least one visitor from abroad, a Paul Hentzner from Germany, who, in 1598, noted that the Prescence Chamber of Queen Elizabeth at Greenwich was 'strewn with hay'.

A slight move towards sophistication was made in the early part of the following century, when a fashion for weaving or plaiting the rushes, diagonally, so as to form 'mats' was introduced. At the same time, trade was developing, with the Turkish or Levant Company, formed towards the end of the 16th century, and a brisk importation of hand-knotted pile carpets and rugs from Smyrna (Izmir), the trading port of the Near East was a natural consequence. These carpets were knotted in the 'manner of Turkey', 'the Turkish Knot', commonly but quite erroneously known as a Ghiordes knot.[2] A fine example of this early type of carpet, plainly made for export to England, can be seen at The Victoria and Albert Museum, inscribed in English: 'Fere God, and keepe his commandments made in the year 1605'. From these luxurious and advanced importations, sprung our own 'Turkey work' so popular in the 17th century. There are several magnificent extant examples of this, one at The Victoria and Albert Museum dated 1672 (See Plate No. 18).

Although the earliest known English needlework carpet is ascribed to about 1550 (see Plate 2), the general practice of embroidering floor coverings did not become common until the early 18th century. The fashion for 'Turkey work' and pile carpets produced in England and imported from the Near East precluded the need for hand-embroidered coverings.

---

[1] Carpets were in use in the Middle East in ancient times. The manufacture of floor coverings was introduced into France by Henri IV, 1589-1610.

[2] See A. Cecil Edwards—*The Persian Carpet* (London 1953) p. 26.

1 English Needlework Carpets

THE ART of embroidery has been known to mankind since the earliest of days. It is usually attributed to the Phrygians, but the Sidonians excelled in it. Embroidery is mentioned in the year 1491 B.C. in the Bible—Exodus XXXV 35 and XXXVIII 23.

In England, embroidery on canvas was known at the time of the Romans and in probability was not so far removed from the 18th century needlework carpets described in this book, although their work was not so grandiose. Research unfortunately, has not produced any real substantiation, but this is fair supposition. From Saxon times, English embroidery was renowned and in the 13th century was unrivalled with the ecclesiastical examples known today as 'Opus Anglicanum'. By this time, canvas embroidery was in fairly general practice. A 13th century English Orfrey preserved at Lyons, has tent-stitch in its construction. Many other examples exist, such as the cope at Pienza and an Orfrey at Lerida in Northern Spain.

There can be little doubt that the making of Spanish needles in this country, first taught by a German, Elias Crowse, in 1566, led to the increased popularity of embroidery as practiced earlier by Mary Queen of Scots, and a little later by Elizabeth Countess of Shrewsbury ('Bess of Hardwick'). Up to then, it would appear that bone needles were in use from early times, for such examples have been found in Saxon remains. Apart from this, some needles were imported in small quantities from Spain.

It seems quite obvious that from the gentle art of embroidering small items for decorative purposes, there evolved the use of larger, more ambitious creations on table or floor, just as pile carpets were being used. The technique of canvas embroidery in itself, justified the use of this type of embroidery for the floor.

Other more delicate forms of embroidery, those not using 'canvas stitches' employing fine silks and metal threads, were obviously by nature unsuitable for the floor.

The needlework with which we are concerned, employed stitches worked on either an open mesh or a closed mesh, to allow the fabric which is used as a foundation to be completely covered with little 'squares' of yarn almost as long as they are broad. This forms on the surface little beads of colour, almost in the same style as pile carpets, and gives a durable finish to the fabric.

During the late 16th century and the first half of the 17th century we do find a few table carpets which it seems logical to assume were not used for floor coverings for the reasons I have already stated in the Introduction.

The middle of the 17th century saw the Great Plague of London, the spread of which was undoubtedly encouraged by the previously mentioned method of 'disposal' of the all-purpose rushes covering the floor. The Great Fire which followed swept away not only old buildings and streets, but also old ideas about fashions, hygiene and homes. Hand-knotted Turkey carpets and their English editions 'Turkey work' gained in popularity.

Probably inspired by a reaction against the austerity of Cromwell's Commonwealth, was the rather over-indulgent practice of putting down rich velvet embroidery 'carpets'. This was an uneconomical and impractical habit, which died out before the end of the century. An example of this type of carpet can be seen at the Victoria and Albert Museum (Museum No. 807-1901).

Before continuing chronologically let us consider the examples of the first half of the 17th century illustrated in this work (Plates No. 9-16). The first thing that we notice is the similarity of design, styling and layout more or less revolving around the composition of the Hulse Carpet (See Plate No. 12). The variation of colour is slight, the work is of a very high standard and the general conception of the work seems to point to a degree of professionalism. When we consider the crudity of the canvas and needles available for use in the home, that such major works as table carpets were attempted, must give us some food for thought, and justify the suspicion that these objects were not worked without some instructed skill. The validity of this is strengthened when the standard and execution of these important items are compared with any example extant of the previous century. The naive simplicity of the latter is very apparent when reference is made to the Oxburgh Hangings of Mary, Queen of Scots, at Oxburgh Hall, Norfolk, and some of the earlier work of Elizabeth, Countess of Shrewsbury, at Hardwick.

It is known that in Elizabethan times, patterns were purchased from the local haberdasher for home embroidery: patterns for gloves, coifs, sleeves, bodices, handkerchiefs etc. It is also known that transfers and sheets of motifs—flowers, insects, birds and animals—were also available for appliqué work. It does not therefore, seem unreasonable to assume that there were some form of prepared canvasses as well. Unfortunately there are not sufficient examples of this period available for a detailed analysis to be made and in spite of diligent research, no definite conclusion can be reached.

Almost at the end of the century another radical change took place, the waning of 'Turkey work' and the introduction of fresh ideas from the Continent. William of Orange, from his native Flanders, brought new styles, habits and customs to England. In Holland it has always been the custom, even to the present day to have table carpets. In the late 17th century there was a substantial production in Delft and Leyden of both embroidered and woven examples, particularly with the floral designs known today as 'tulip carpets or tapestry'. It is a small step from the needlework upholstered chairs, fashionable toward the end of the century and the beginning of the 18th to needlework table covers and floor coverings.

This idea, which started in a small way at the turn of the century, snowballed into a profusion of beautiful, decorative, well-balanced carpets in the first half of the

18th century. This fifty years produced the artistic peak in English needlework carpets, with their superb colour, quality and craftsmanship. A prime example is at Hatfield House, the property of the Marquess of Salisbury (See Plate No. 34).

There seems however to be ample evidence to support the theory that in the 18th century, needlework carpets and rugs had quite an element of professional production about them, and were not simply, as has been widely held, the work of ladies of the house, who embroidered to pass away the time. This is not to say that such leisure activity did not take place. A most famous signed example of first class domestic work is the Holte Carpet (Plate No. 40).

However, in the early 1950's I came across an English example of about 1735 (Plate No. 28), worked in polychrome wools, in cross-stitch on canvas. It was worked with a floral design. At the instigation of a well-known London dealer who acquired it from me, we removed the cheap cotton lining. Along the canvas selvedge at various intervals, could still be seen swatches of wools in the various colours employed in the embroidering of this carpet. The canvas upon which the work had been carried out, showed, where worn, ample evidence of stencilling. It may even have been the painting or drawing of the designs. Wherever this carpet was worn, these lines showed, clearly sketched on the canvas.

Similarly, Mrs. Owen Compton-Bracebridge, says she spent one whole winter in restoring and repairing the Holte Carpet (Plate No. 40), before it was sold to the City of Birmingham Museum and Art Gallery. When repairing it, she wondered how it had been worked. Was it designed by an artist? Did they have squared paper in the 1740's? She did notice, however, that there was a faint stencilling on the canvas indicating the pattern, as though it had been marked out on the canvas.

Taking into account the continuity and flow of the designs, the similarity in the rendering, and the choice of the very profuse flowers employed, it seems very likely that stencilled canvases, complete with wool swatches were sold to the general public.

Hence the existence of dated and signed examples worked perhaps in the manor or house, by the ladies of the house. But the execution and the very high standard attained seems to suggest, too, that there may have been small private workshops where these canvases could be executed on a professional basis. In time, perhaps, evidence will appear which will establish this beyond doubt.

Meanwhile, another change was developing, in outlook and thinking, and this inevitably led, once again to change in the manner of covering floors. In 1735, the weaving of double-cloth carpeting at Kidderminster and later at Wilton, preceded the advent of machine-made floor coverings. 1778 saw the establishment of a factory at Kilmarnock and in 1839 'Axminster' production commenced. The industry was helped by the importation of jute in small quantities, in 1795; by the 1820's it was being imported in large quantities and adopted for carpet making.

In the year 1750, artisans who were extremely discontented with conditions at the

Savonnerie workshops at Gobelins, left France and re-established the manufacture of hand-knotted carpets in England. An Englishman, Thomas Moore, won an award from the Royal Society of Arts in 1757 for his skill in making these hand-made pile carpets. Lady Mary Coke in 1768 gave a full account of his work.

The Adam Brothers, who much admired Thomas Moore's work, designed and used his Moorfields carpets through the last quarter of the century. This revival of hand knotted pile carpets, together with the prevailing Classical decor in vogue, once again almost eliminated the production of needlework carpets. It seems to be proven beyond doubt, for I have not been able to trace any examples of this period.

The invention of the Jacquard Loom by Joseph Marie Jacquard in 1801, and its introduction into England in the early part of the 19th century, greatly increased and cheapened the cost of manufacture of 'Brussels' carpeting in Norwich and Bradford. This invention, allied to James Watts' invention of the steam engine, led to the establishment of machine looms at Kidderminster in 1825.

With the increasing use of machines, the 19th century saw trends being adapted, altered and disbanded with alarming rapidity. The importation of 'Berlin woolwork' created a revival and demand once again for needlework carpets and rugs. Due to the rapid developments in the invention of aniline dyes, colours became crude and harsh. These were somewhat modified and improved by the dyers, as they acquainted themselves with their new-found means of expression.

The departure from formal and floral patterns in embroidery brought in a spate of subjects depicting the Royal Family, portraits of notable personages of the day, and even liturgical figures and scenes. Since the embroidery was used for either floor coverings or seat coverings, the Church and the general public became incensed against such allegedly disrespectful, or even blasphemous practices, and an outcry for the discontinuation of such work was inevitable. Thus, once more, needlework carpets and rugs slipped from high fashion almost into oblivion.

2 Recognition and Identification

WHILST preparing this book, I have had so many examples submitted for inclusion that have been incorrectly described, that I decided to include a brief introduction to recognition and identification. To go into this subject fully would take much more discussion and chapters than it is possible to include in this work, but in order to help the reader establish recognition I have attempted to cover all aspects in a brief survey.

It is quite understandable that many readers confuse needlework of Continental provenance with English needlework. Let us begin, therefore, by establishing what is actually meant by needlework. It is embroidery carried out in either wool, silk or some other thread, worked on canvas made either from linen, cotton, jute, hemp, or any other material. The stitches employed being universal, such as tent-stitch, cross-stitch, etc., does not in itself provide an indication.

Bearing this in mind, it is easy to see that floral designs, animal designs, geometrical designs—in fact any design—would appear to the uninitiated as being just this, with apparently no clue as to where or when it was made. But there are many differences in fact which, when pointed out, will be more easily identifiable and which will put the reader along the right road to establishing recognition.

MID 16th CENTURY TO FIRST HALF 17th CENTURY
(Plates Nos. 2-16)

ENGLISH. Examples of this period are table carpets, mostly with Italian Renaissance designs probably coming to England via Flanders. They invariably portray scrolling, with varieties of flowers, animals, houses, and figures, in the style and costume of the period. The layout of the designs have delicate grace and movement, and are more simple and naive than the Continental versions. The flowers represented are obviously those commonly found in this country. The animals are usually heraldic or legendary beasts, depicted in imaginative hunting scenes. Castles or houses can mostly be identified with contemporary architecture. As there was a great difference in dress between this country and the Continent, attention should be paid to costume, in particular ladies' dress.

In common with the Continent we had ruffs, hoops and wired hair styles, but the skirts here were definitely 'barrel' shape. This continued in a modified form until the end of the first quarter of the 17th century when it gave way to the simpler, yet somehow richer style of Charles I. Men's dress too, with its trunk hose showing through the opening of the trunks, boots held up by leather straps, breeches in Venetian (full) or

14

French (tight) style and cape in the Italian fashion were very different from contemporary Continental fashion. In the first quarter of the 17th century breeches became loose with ribbons at the knees. The jacket had stiffened, the cape lengthened, and reaction had set in towards simplicity and against the prissy points and bunches of ribbons of the preceding era.

If the example being considered has crests, identification of coats-of-arms with English families is another very strong indication, though not an infallible rule, as work was commissioned abroad occasionally for English use. The colours in general use were usually greens, blues, yellows, reds (brick). English dyes from the beginning of the 17th century onwards gave a clear and deep hue. The colours were fresh and have not faded a great deal. On the reverse they retain their original tints with very slight patination. It is interesting to note that up to about 1608 fine wools were sent to Holland for dyeing and that in 1628 two dyers were flogged for teaching their art in the North of England. In 1783 an act was passed against 'abuses in dyeing'.

The wools employed in English examples have a springy and silky touch and are reputed from earliest times to be the best in the world. Wool manufactures are mentioned in the year 1185, but it was not really until John Kempe introduced wool weaving in the year 1331 that it became noteworthy. Again it is interesting to note that the exportation of wool was prohibited in 1696, the act being passed in the year 1718 and not repealed until 1824.

CONTINENTAL. Very often the Continental interpretation of design, though from a similar basic source, is complicated and sophisticated. Technically lack of definition is alleviated by the use of outline. More formal designs were favoured, giving a more stylized and staider effect. Flowers common to the Continent are more profuse and varied, and this is reflected in the design. Buildings and architecture are frequently imposing and forthright in the late Renaissance and early Baroque taste. Ladies skirts—which are not so accentuated as the English 'barrel' shape—fall away from the bodice in a more gentle line. Men's dress too, is detectably different. Where crests occur, it can be ascertained if these are of Continental origin. The colours, usually greens, blues, faded yellows, sometimes faded brick, are similar to the English up to the beginning of the 17th century. From then onwards they have lost colour more easily, they lack the freshness and depth of the English, and it can be seen on the reverse side where the yellows and other colours have noticeably faded. The wools employed are much coarser and rougher to the touch, and lack the springiness and silken texture of English wools.

1700-1800—ENGLISH

In order to avoid repetition I should like to make it quite clear that throughout this century, remarks that I have already made concerning the layout of design, in English needlework, the clarity of design, the absence of outline, the identification of coats-of-arms, the details of costumes etc., still apply. The wool still is silken in texture and

15

springy and the same still applies to the depth and definition of colour. Where colour is concerned, the fields of the carpets in this era are usually on a blue ground (see colour Plate No. 34), sometimes brown or sometimes coral. Very seldom red and rarely yellow. The yellow used in English examples has a distinctive hue, akin to Chinese yellow: that is, it has a lot of green in it, and when faded it tones down to a pleasant buff. At the beginning of the century a deep violet almost like a 'blackish purple' was in use. Later, this same colour was not so 'blackish'. In both cases, however, the colour fades away leaving a 'bluish-white' on the face side. On the reverse side it naturally still shows this very fresh dark 'purplish' colour. This is a peculiarity of this particular English dye at this period.

BAROQUE (CHINOISERIE) With the ascension of William of Orange and Mary in 1688, fashion changed. The Dutch flower painters of the 17th century, the Brueghels, and the Bosschaerts in the early part of the century and Jan Van Huysum and Rachel Ruysch in the late 17th or early part of the 18th century had left their mark. The Dutch Colonies in the Far East had, by the end of the 17th century, contributed to the Italian designs of the Dutch Baroque which filtered into England.

Starting with a more simple form at the turn of the century, we see under Queen Anne (1702-1714) a strong development of the Baroque Chinoiserie. A mixture of large exotic blooms, hydrangeas, peonies, chrysanthemums, carnations etc., combining with a remaining vestige of the Jacobean leaf pattern. Ladies' dress has changed, she now wears a very large hoop, with the consequence that her skirt is enormous, her hair is set in a more natural fashion. He now wears a long jacket with a long waistcoat, wide cuffs ending in lace frills. Animals, too, have become more naturalistic, although the naive 'Carolean stumpwork' type of interpretation is still met with. (See Plate No. 19.)

The second and third decade of the century saw a more vigorous style. Masses of flowers, arranged sometimes in the manner of the Indian Palampores, calicos, 'pintados' and chintzes. Indian influence was very strong at this time, so much so that Parliament in the year 1700, having banned the importation of Indian calicos and chintzes because they were ruining the silk industry, in 1721 extended the ban to all cotton goods. In 1736 the law was relaxed. The demand for 'Indianeries' as seen in the Soho Tapestries[1] of 1700-1730, the japanned and lacquered furniture with Indian motifs, called erroneously 'Chinoiserie' together with the general decor of this time, showed that the desire and demand for this type of decor was very strong indeed. Consequently designs at home followed this trend very closely. (See Plates No. 23, 24, 26, 27, 30, 38.)

CLASSICAL MOVEMENT. Around the early 1720's, there appeared a school of designers and architects, to whom the heavy pomp of Baroque was an anathema. Led by the great patron Burlington, and practised by William Kent, they sought again the

---

[1] See Plate 13 (A. & B.) *English Tapestries of the 18th Century*. H. C. Marillier, London, 1930.

purity of Italian Renaissance, derived from designs by Andrea Palladio. The Raby Carpet (Plate No. 25) is a very fine example of this style, which was destined to have only a very short existence.

THE ROCOCO. La Rocaille from Les Rocailleurs, emanated in France about the year 1700 and dominated Europe until about the end of the third quarter of the century. By the end of the fourth decade it was showing itself strongly in England. It reached its zenith in the mid 1750's and continued in a declining fashion until the mid 1760's to reappear again in the early 19th century. This stylized and distorted assymetry, with its renunciation of straight lines, its perplexingly entangled curves shows itself very clearly in this period (See Plates No. 39, 41, 42). It can best be recognized by its 'C' curves, its twists and its turns.

CHINOISERIE. Parallel to the Rococo and even long before it, there developed a taste for the Far East, a taste for everything to be in the manner of the Chinese. This, no doubt, was brought about by travel, by books, and by the East India Trading Company. It was, in fact, brought about by a general ignorance of the Orient. The taste for 'Chinoiserie', a word coined for the free and fantastic European conception of Chinese taste in all branches of the arts, subsided during the early Georgian period, to return to favour towards the end of the fifth decade, during the reign of George II, and to reach its peak in the year 1754 with the publication of Chippendale's Director.[1] It faded away with the appearance of the Neo-classical trend, to re-appear in the 19th century, with George, Prince of Wales, and to continue in a less charming, and much more ornate fashion until about 1830 (See Plates No. 44, 45, 50).

THE NEO-CLASSICISM. A revolt against the excesses and frivolities of the Rococo. The period of the Adam Brothers which developed in the late 1760's to wane about the year 1800. The probable reasons for my being unable to find any examples of English needlework carpets of this period I deal with elsewhere.

THE GOTHIC REVIVAL. The name given to that style of decoration and design introduced by the construction of Strawberry Hill, in the middle of the 18th century, by Horace Walpole, and furnished with the help of his Committee of Taste. It was the rising of a new order and continued until its decline with the sale of the contents of Strawberry Hill in 1842. It was as its name implies an attempt to revive and combine medieval styling and decoration with classical backgrounds (See Plates No. 56, 57, 71).

1700—1800 CONTINENTAL

Dealing with Continental examples of this century, obviously a great stress must be placed on France. A possible explanation for a comparative lack of French examples could be that at the French Court, it was the custom of the ladies and nobles of the day to spend their continual time at the court for the 'levees' etc. This naturally prevented the ladies and their husbands from attending to the decor of their estates and perhaps

[1]Chippendale, Thomas, *Gentleman & Cabinet Makers Director*, 1754.

too, denied them the time to indulge in canvas embroidery, which is arduous and takes time and room, particularly in the case of floor coverings.

The introduction by Louis XIV *le Roi Soleil* of the hand-knotted pile carpets 'in the manner of Turkey' at the Gobelins soapworks—known as *La Savonnerie*—led to poor imitations known as *point noué*, literally knotted stitch. Similarly the Aubusson and Felletin tapestry factories in the Marche country, at the time of the Regency, Louis XV and Louis XVI, began to manufacture Aubusson or tapestry-weave carpets, which were produced in great numbers throughout the century and continued up to the end of the third quarter of the 19th century. Thus these reasons, together with the rather silky, plush decor which would be somewhat out of character with needlework carpets, would probably account for the rarity of floor coverings in needlework. Occasionally a *tapis de table* or a *dessus de lit*, or perhaps some curtains[1] are encountered.

However Madame de Maintenon—wife of Louis XIV—founded the school or Institute of Embroidery, which afterwards became the Convent of St. Cyr. To this school, the nobility of France and Europe in general, sent their daughters to learn the gentle art of embroidery and in particular that canvas embroidery which today is known as *Point de St. Cyr*. This would account for the similarity in design all over the Continent, in Italy, Austria, Holland, Belgium, Switzerland, etc. It is known, too, that the Netherlands was sending her patterns to Spain. Up to the turn of the century, the designs in general use were based on the Chinoiserie designs of Apollo-Louis (Louis XIV) influenced by Mme. de Maintenon and La Compagnie des Indes.

Bearing in mind that the arts were under the influence of Berain, Audran, Watteau, Huet, Le Prince, Boucher and Pillement, it is very easily understandable how 'Chinoiserie' ran almost through the entire century, a much more protracted and intense influence than in England. Allied to this was 'La Rocaille'. This assymetric scrolling which dominated Continental design throughout the first three-quarters of the century showed itself in every conceivable fashion and manner. In fact combined with Chinoiserie it ran riot with its 'singeries' and its monkeys. In the 1770's, Jean Pillement in revolt against the seemingly eternal rocaille, and drawing inspiration no doubt from Madame de Pompadour and Francois Boucher, introduced once again decor in the manner of the Far East. His exotic landscapes and birds, rockeries, flowers and trees did much to dispel the strong hold of the rocaille. The last quarter saw a change in fashion and dress, with the consequence that at first small designs, popular in Italy at the beginning of the 17th century, were re-introduced and the century closed with the Directoire, and revival of classical design.

Once again we must look to the general layout of design and see if it lacks in definition, if it is more complicated and lacking in naturalness. The quality of the wool is coarse and harsh to the touch except for a short period from about 1765-1815 when it became

[1] See Y. Hackenbroch, *English and other Needlework in the Irwin Untermyer Collection*, New York, 1960, page 60.

18

soft and fleecy. This was due no doubt to the importation of wool from the merino sheep from Saxony. Crests and buildings have to be studied and compared with their English equivalents. Colour too, which is very important, is less deep and fresh than in England. The yellows are of a more mustardy hue and fade to a butter tinge. The purple which fades to a 'bluish-white' is not in common usage and on the reverse shows more as a 'bluish-purple' rather than the blackish of the English variety. For the first half of the century, the flowers in vogue and most popular are *Les Pavos*—an exotic interpretation of the red poppy.

Again the importance of recognising costume cannot be stressed too much. It is very different from the English costume of the same time, with its fontanges[1], its adriennes[1] and its falballas[1]. Later in the century, its panniers and hairstyles developed until the time of Louis XVI there were created the luxuriant but preposterous hairstyles, peculiar to this period in France and much lampooned by caricaturists of the period. Hats, too, reached a time when there were perhaps a hundred different styles in vogue such as *La Tarare*, *l'Espagnole*, *l'Anglomane* and *La Belle Poule*[2]. From the 1760's women's dress was made to part in a triangle from the waist and made to fit over the large panniers. These dresses were known as *la robe a la Francaise*.

From about 1770 onwards these panniers were dispensed with and reacting against the stiff, hampering mode there emerged *la robe a la Polonnaise* which sloped gently from the waist and loosely towards the back, to be drawn back into a bustle by buttons and loops of ribbons puffed out at the hips. This developed at the end of the century to the high waist and style known as 'the Directoire' style. Men's costume is very different from the English, too, being very much richer and more fussy and governed by statutory laws until after the Revolution when it is less fussy, simpler and more practical.

1800—1900   ENGLISH

The nineteenth century was a period of great activity, change and experiment. Robert Adam, whose designs had so dominated the latter part of the 18th century had died, and his classical tradition was carried on by Nash, Holland and William Porden. Deterioration set in, as was inevitable, originality and good taste were often forsaken, giving way, particularly later in the century, to banal and tasteless apeing and reproduction. This early period saw the construction of Carlton House, Regent Street and Brighton Pavilion.

The Gothic revival (See Plates No. 56, 57, 58, 59, 71), together with the continuation of the Classical and Chinoiserie styles (See Plates No. 67, 73), continued up to the beginning of the Victorian age. A contemporary development was the re-introduction

---

[1]Fontage (top knot); Falballas (flounces); Adriennes (low-cut long dresses made of flimsy silks or light satins to accentuate movement, and shape of the body and limbs. See Paul Lacroix, *The 18th Century, its Institutions, Customs and Costumes*, France, 1700-1789.

[2]Lacroix, p. 477, figs. 1, 2, 4; p. 479, figs. 3 and 5.

of the style of Louis XVI (See Plate No. 66). In the early 1820's there was a diluted and strongly adapted return to the rococo scrollings. This somewhat half-hearted reversion remained until the 1840's (See Plates No. 61, 62, 63, 64, 65, 70).

We now come to the Victorian era, 1837-1901. In all fairness it must be stressed that 'Victorian' is by no means synonymous with 'ugly', but the unavoidable departure from natural, ingenuous handcraft, generally indicated a decline in individual standards of design and workmanship. Referring to our own subject a radical change of approach to the working of needlework carpets came about in the early part of the century. In Berlin about the year 1810, a Mr. Wittich first published designs, printed or painted on squared paper for the embroidery of coloured wools on canvas squares. These squares were transferred into needlework, by counting the number of squares on the paper and, using the appropriate colour, taking up a similar number of squares on the canvas and embroidering them accordingly. The squares were then joined, and the desired number was finished off by a border.

By 1830 these complete sets (comprising paper, canvas squares and coloured wools), were being imported into this country in ever increasing numbers by Mr. Wilks of Regent Street. The wools employed were manufactured in Gotha and dyed in Berlin. Thus the name Berlin woolwork was adapted. At first, glass beads were incorporated into the designs, but later this idea was dropped, in England at least. The fashion remained popular for the greater part of the century and in due course these squares were made here. The 1830's also saw the introduction of bleached canvas and canvas squares with two-size mesh in the same piece, which facilitated the embroidery of Berlin woolwork. A little later the designs were stencilled or printed direct on to the canvas. With the squares were given detailed instructions for working, similar to present day knitting, giving in either letter or number form, the stitches, colours of wools, and so on, to be employed.

By the opening of the Victorian era, large flowers were already popular. In the 1840's scrolls, cartouches and architectural designs were being introduced into the floral patterns. (See Plates No. 69, 70, 71, 79). Another design to make its mark during these ten years was the imitation of Caucasian carpet designs (See Plate No. 77). The 'stained glass' design carpets were a hangover from the effects of the Gothic revival period. (See Plate No. 71). By the late 1840's convolvulus, hydrangeas and striped tulips were being used. At the same time, a rather delightful series of carpets, made up of small very finely worked squares (kettle holders) sometimes joined to larger squares were embroidered. These often depicted landscapes, animals, or small typical scenes from contemporary life. (See Plates No. 74, 75, 76, 78).

The Great Exhibition at Crystal Palace in 1851 heralded competitions in designs inaugurated by The Royal Society of Arts. From this sprang yet another fancy. For the sake of convenience I have named these examples 'Tile Carpets'. (See Plates Nos. 82–86). From 1860, Victorian design, as most people think of it, had really got under way.

Large exaggerated flowers, sometimes with a fern design, sprawled gracelessly in harsh colours; and yet undeniably striking. (See Plates No. 88, 89, 91). In 1870, large cabbage roses, exotic flowers, lillies, orchids and the passion flower, combined in huge profusions of colour to provide the mainstay of late Victorian needlework carpet designs. (See Plates No. 87, 92). Of course there were off-shoots and reactions. In the 1880's this showed itself in 'The Queen Anne' revival. Another style featured huge sunflowers and peacock's feathers. (See Plate No. 93).

The quality of wool varied during the century. From 1824 the export ban on home produced wools was lifted, with the result that the wool for home use lost some of its exceptional quality. Another factor in the decline was the importation of German wools for the Berlin Woolwork. The imported wool was of an inferior quality, and dyed in harsh colours. Later the situation improved, and home produced wools regained much of their 18th century quality.

Colours too, varied enormously. We start the century with natural or vegetable dyes, but the Unverdorben discovery of aniline dyes in 1826, brought an incredible change. This discovery led to an introduction of colour ranges not thought of before, so that by the middle of the century, graduation of colour and elaborate shading of floral designs, made the designs almost stand out in naturalistic relief. This was the height of attainment of the 19th century carpets. It is noticeable too, that until the middle of the century, the use of black ground for a carpet was an uncommon ocurrence, whereas from then on it would seem to become general use.

In 1835 the first solid green was used. Dr. Stenhouse in 1848 was instrumental in Mr. Marnas obtaining mauve from lichens. It was not until 1856 that Mr. H. W. Perkin (later knighted) showed how a violet oxidation-product (mauve) could be supplied in dyeing. This produced purple. Dr. Hoffman's production of aniline dyes from coal tar, led to the manufacture of mauve, red, nightgreen and black. In 1861 aniline blue and in 1863 aniline magenta were introduced. In 1869 alizarine colours, from a madder base, discovered by Robinquet and Cohn in 1831, were in general use, synthetic indigo first made its appearance in 1897.

1800—1900 CONTINENTAL

As far as France was concerned, tapestry weave carpets from Aubusson, and *point noue* carpets generally excluded the use of needlework. Some exceptions may be found however, made for church use as altar carpets by the convents, or for use in the convents themselves. Ecclesiastical medallions or motifs, with or without floral appendages, make these easily identifiable. The rest of the continent generally continued to look to France for design interpretations.

The first twenty years of the century saw a few needlework carpets and rugs. These, in the main, were copied from the Aubusson designs of the Napoleonic and Restoration periods, which were strongly influenced by Napoleon's triumphs in Egypt.

The revival of the styles of Louis XIV, Louis XV and Louis XVI started in the 1820's and continued up to about the 1860's. The Musée des Arts Decoratifs in Paris, built in the 1860's, was initiated primarily to provide antique pieces for copying. Original design had deteriorated to that extent. In the 1860's there was introduced 'Japonaiserie' designs of small butterflies, birds and small flowers in the taste of Kakiemon porcelain.

The exportation of Berlin woolwork to Holland, Belgium, Switzerland, Italy, Spain and Portugal, provided a field of production of the type common in England. There are differences between that produced here and the continent. Layout, colour and wool are indications together with a study of costume where possible and the indistinct definition. Invariably the designs on black grounds or harsh light grounds, with garish purples, and hard yellows were most popular in Germany, Those with architectural embellishments in the floral motif, or surrounding the motif, with vine leaves, grapes, etc., can usually be attributed to France. Although, originally all the designs for Berlin woolwork stemmed from Germany, each country had preferences according to its national taste.

3 Stitches

In English needlework carpets and rugs, the stitches most frequently employed were

Tent Stitch or Petit Point.

Tent-stitch (so called because formerly embroidery on a frame was referred to as tent work) or petit-point. The finest of the canvas stitches. In English form, usually worked in diagonal lines across the canvas. In the Continental form usually worked in horizontal rows.

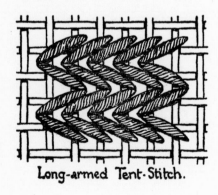

Cross Stitch

Cross-stitch or gros-point. The most common of all the canvas stitches. In English form, the final crossing stitch must always be in the same direction. Hence this gives added strength. On the reverse, it forms 'with a little imagination', a sort of chain effect peculiar only to English work, and hardly any canvas shows. In the Continental form, on the reverse the canvas shows easily, it is not thick to the feel, and has the appearance of straight lines.

Long-armed Tent-Stitch.

Long-armed tent-stitch—a variation of tent-stitch. Another variation is called reverse tent-stitch, which gives a striped or chevron effect. Reference is sometimes made to crewel-work stitch—this is only a variation of long and short stitch, in itself a variation of tent-stitch.

23

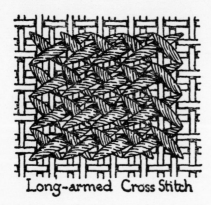

Long-armed Cross Stitch

Long-armed Cross-stitch or Greek stitch. On the reverse side it usually has two parallel lines of back stitch.

As we are concerned with carpets and rugs, it is usual to find English examples worked with one of the foregoing, with perhaps occasionally French knots in the centre of the flowers. Of course where smaller items were concerned, many other canvas stitches were used.

In addition to the modified forms of tent-stitch and cross-stitch, the following stitches were also in common use on the Continent for carpets and rugs.

A. *Straight or upright cross-stitch.*

Usually to be found in French, German and Dutch examples.

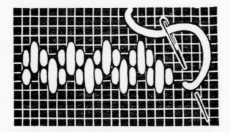

B. *Hungarian stitch.*

Commonly used in Italian examples worked in silks—rarely in wools, except in Spanish examples.

C. *Rice or William and Mary stitch.*

Used frequently for the backgrounds of Dutch examples.

24

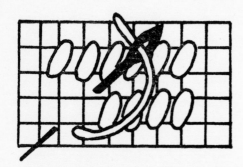

D. *Gobelin stitch.*

Usually seen in French work and late German and Austrian work.

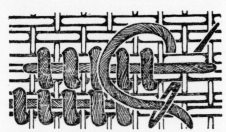

E. *Upright Gobelin stitch.*

Usually seen on French examples and coarse Austrian pieces. Similar to the Gobelin stitch, except that sometimes one or two threads are laid along the canvas. There is a diagonal variation too.

Flemish work of the late 16th and 17th centuries was invariably carried out entirely in tent-stitch or a composition of cross-stitch and tent-stitch—Continental type.

Canvas. The canvas used, regardless of texture or thread (jute, hemp, linen), was of uniform mesh up to the first quarter of the 19th century.

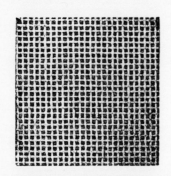

Cotton canvas was in use in Turkey (from Adana) and in the Middle East, from the end of the 17th century, and probably before this. Early 18th century Daghestan needlework table covers, pillow and bolster cases were worked on fine cotton canvas. However, it was not until the 1830's in England, when bleaching of canvas was introduced, that cotton canvases were beginning to be used. The reason for the long delay before the development of cotton canvases reached England have been previously explained.

Also at this time Double thread mesh was gaining popularity. This was (and in fact, still is) a canvas where the warps were so arranged that on one piece of canvas there were two different sizes of mesh. This, together with other reasons that have already been mentioned, speeded up the embroidering of Berlin woolwork.

NEEDLES. Bone needles have been found in Saxon remains. It is interesting to note that the making of Spanish needles was first taught in England by a German, Elias Crowse, *circa* 1566.

JOINING UP. Since a number of 'made-up' or 'joined-up' examples are on sale, particularly of the 19th century, it is felt that a word should be said concerning this process. A number of carpets are of course 'original', in the sense that they have neither been added to, nor detracted from since their incipience, other than restorations or reparations due to normal wear and tear. The majority of 19th century examples encountered however, are made up from either borders removed from Victorian curtains, or from 19th century plush table covers, or from bell-pulls. Sometimes odd squares of Berlin woolwork have been employed. In the 18th century (particularly in the Continental examples) screen panels, bed-curtains, and wall hangings have often been joined together and made to look like original carpets and rugs. This also applies in a lesser degree to the 17th century. Such panels, when made up at the present time, are invisibly sewn together on the *surface* (face-side). This can be immediately detected. The correct way of joining is by taking the two selvedges on the *back*, sewing them together in back stitch. The selvedges are then opened out and pressed flat. Occasionally if the seams or the canvas show on the face side it may be necessary to 'overwork' a line or two of embroidery to complement the design.

Descriptive Notes
on the Illustrations

PLATE 1   THE LUTTRELL TABLE CARPET   18ft. 1in. by 6ft. 4in.
1st Quarter 16th Century—c. 1520
BY COURTESY OF THE GLASGOW MUSEUMS AND ART GALLERIES
(THE SIR WILLIAM BURRELL COLLECTIONS)

This rare and important Tudor example, from the time of Henry VIII, is perhaps the earliest known English table carpet. It is tapestry woven, and like the 'Lewkenor' example (Plate 3) is included for the sake of completeness. It commemorates the marriage of Sir Andrew Luttrell of Dunster and Quantoxhead, and Margaret, daughter of Sir Thomas Wyndham of Felbrigg, Norfolk, whose arms form the centre. The colour of the field is black with light green in the borders. The border shields are said to represent (1) Beaumont; (2) Courtenay; (3) Luttrell and Audley; (4) Luttrell and Hill; (5) Luttrell and Wyndham; (6) Luttrell and Hill; (7) Luttrell and Wyndham; (8) Luttrell and Hill; (9) Luttrell and Audley; (10) Wyndham, Scrope and Tibetot; (11) Luttrell and Beaumont; (12) Courtenay.

Its design has a lot in common with the designs used in some early silken stuff in the Mauresque style from Granada. In the Kunstgewerbe Museum, Berlin, there is a panel of this type of silk attributed to Spain 15th century, with a polygonal pattern which is almost identical with the central field of this carpet excluding the coat of arms.[1]

coll.   In 1580 bequeathed by Dame Margaret Luttrell to her daughter, who married Peter Edgcumbe of Mount Edgcumbe.
         It thus passed into the possession of Lord Mount Edgcumbe of Cotehell House, Cornwall.
         Later acquired by Mr. Howard Carter.
         Sir William Burrell purchased it in the late 1920's or early 1930's.

N.B.   *In the light of recent research by the Metropolitan Museum of Art, New York, it has been virtually established that both the Lewkenor and the Luttrell tapestry table carpets were worked in Flemish ateliers, to designs sent from England. Bearing in mind that we are fundamentally concerned with English carpet design and its development, these two examples are deliberately not being omitted.*

PLATE 2   THE GIFFORD CARPET   18ft. 4in. by 4ft. 6in.
2nd Quarter 16th Century—c. 1550
BY COURTESY OF THE VICTORIA AND ALBERT MUSEUM

This earliest known English needlework carpet was acquired by the Victoria and Albert Museum in 1930 (Museum ref. T.151-1930), with the help of the National Art Collections Fund. It is entirely worked in tent stitch, in polychrome wools on a linen canvas. There are about twenty stitches to the inch, which corresponds approximately to 400 knots to the inch in a pile carpet—an exceedingly fine texture. The field covered with a small geometrical diaper on a yellow ground, has on it three circular panels enclosed in wreaths of flowers and acorns. The central panel with probably the arms of Gifford, is flanked on each side with a medallion containing a stag under an oak tree. The main

---

[1] Otto von Falke—*Decorative Silks*. Fig. 315

27

border in a conventional floral design has on each side a narrower geometrical stripe. The composition of this carpet, a small patterned field, with three circular medallions containing figuration and enclosed in wreaths, is very akin to the design of the stylised mille-fleurs tapestry of circa 1475 attributed to the Rhine Basin. Traditionally associated with Lady Margaret Beaufort, Countess of Richmond and Derby (1443-1509), whose mother was the widow of Sir Oliver St. John of Bletsoe; until supported by more conclusive evidence, it is better to date it as from the middle of the 16th century.

coll.   Lord St. John of Bletsoe.
repr.   A. F. Kendrick—*English Decorative Fabrics of the 16th to 18th Centuries*. Plate 3.
          Symonds & Preece—*Needlework thro' the Ages*. Plate 39.
lit.   C. E. C. Tattersall—*A History of British Carpets*, p.99.

PLATE 3   THE LEWKENOR TABLE CARPET   16ft. 3in. by 7ft. 5in.
                    3rd Quarter 16th Century—c. 1564
              BY COURTESY OF THE METROPOLITAN MUSEUM OF ART, NEW YORK

A rare and important Elizabethan Armorial tapestry table carpet dated ANO.DNI 1564. There is no armorial table carpet of the 16th century which bears comparison with this panel. This of course, is tapestry woven, possibly of Netherlandish or more likely Flemish work,[1] and it is included with the Luttrell Carpet for the sake of continuity and comparison. The central shield bears the arms of Sir Roger Lewkenor and his wife Elizabeth Messent. Perhaps W. G. Thomson's description from *A History of Tapestry Weaving in England* deals more than adequately with it . . . . . 'Another tapestry, probably made at Barcheston, *contains the arms and alliances of the Lewkenor family. The central coat is enclosed by a wreath, with boy supporters who stand on a mound on which are cowslips, wild strawberries, heartsease, and other flowers, against a dark background almost covered by a less natural spray of flowers, like lillies, roses and honeysuckles. The border is composed of bunches of flowers and fruit, amongst which are arranged fourteen armorials of the family alliances.* Originally at West Dene, Sussex, the tapestry was brought to Chawton Manor in 1737. Its purpose was explained in a memorandum of 1662 in the handwriting of Sir John Lewkenor: '*Remember to keep safe the carpet of arms, now aged about 100 years, which in the failure of the older house totalie consuming itself by daughters and heires and passing into other names, was sent hither by Constance Glemham of Trotton, who was one of those heires, for record to the younger house and whole name*'. It is the ancestral property of Montagu George Knight, of Chawton Manor, Herts, and is dated 1564.

coll.   Frank Partridge & Sons Ltd., London.
auct.   Sotheby & Co., London.
lit.   W. G. Thomson—*Tapestry Weaving in England*, p.52.
          W. G. Thomson—*A History of Tapestry*, pp.267-268, illus.

PLATE 4   Size 9ft. by 9ft.
              Rare ELIZABETHAN TABLE COVER (or bedspread)
                    4th Quarter 16th Century—c. 1580
                  BY COURTESY THE MARQUESS OF SALISBURY

Amongst the valuable treasures at Hatfield House, is this exquisite needlework table carpet. It is of delightful colouring and symmetrical design, and is worked in polychrome wools, in tent-stitch, cross-stitch and chain-stitch on four strips of canvas.
The central field on a beige background is composed of alternate rows of stylized octagonal peonies

---

[1] See comment to the Luttrell Carpet, plate 1, p. 27.

and libate floral motifs, enclosed within a diamond shaped pattern. It is worked in a great variety of natural colours: China blue, rose, black, gold, sage green and terra-cotta. The libate floral motifs are similar in character to the backcloth of a seated figure in one of the series of the 'Apocalypse' tapestries woven at Angers 1375-84 and now at The Musée des Tapisseries, Angers. This is also reminiscent of the stylised patterns employed by Elizabeth Countess of Shrewsbury in her 16th century embroidered panel exhibited at The Franco British Exhibition of Textiles at the Victoria and Albert Museum in 1921 (No. 204).

The most interesting border has tudor roses alternating with vases and arabesque floral motifs, on a terracotta ground, worked in rose, blue and magenta.

From the poor join in the centre, it can be seen that this superb example was larger at one time. Mr. L. W. Shea, the curator at Hatfield House, tells me that there were a number of roundels which bore certain lettering. It was difficult to decipher these inscriptions, but one he remembers read 'The clowds do hyde the starres'.

This carpet originally embroidered by members of the family, has been in the possession of the Cecils since it was first completed. It is highly probable that it belonged originally to Lord Burghley,[1] the father of Robert Cecil,[2] the first Earl of Salisbury.

PLATE 5   ELIZABETHAN CARPET   9ft. 5in. by 4ft. 10in.

4th Quarter 16th Century—c.1600

BY COURTESY OF THE VICTORIA AND ALBERT MUSEUM

This carpet (Museum No. T.41-1928) might have been used on table or floor and probably dates from the late 16th or very early 17th century. It is worked in polychrome wools on a linen canvas, entirely in long-armed cross-stitch. There are about 13 rows to the inch, corresponding approximately to a pile carpet with 170 knots to the square inch. The field has a pattern of alternately light and dark octagonal panels containing geometrical tracery which is clearly derived from a Turkish design, similar to that in the well known 'Holbein' carpets. The diamond-shaped interspaces are filled with sprigs of roses, pansies and thistles on a green ground. The border has a modification of the Eastern Cufic pattern on a blue ground. The colour scheme is worked with shades of blue, green and purple as well as black, and yields a rich, deep, greenish effect. Several carpets of this kind are illustrated by De Farcy,[3] who attributes to them a French origin. The present example is ascribed to England chiefly on account of the characteristic rendering as well as choice of flowers. These may be compared with Plate XXXVI (illustration 203) Victoria and Albert Museum, The Franco-British Exhibition of Textiles, 1921,[4] and Plate XXXVII (illustrations 105-106) of the same book. The first illustration bears the embroidered monogram of Mary Queen of Scots, and the latter two are ascribed to Elizabeth Countess of Shrewsbury (1520-1607). These three embroidered canvas panels are in the collection of the Duke of Devonshire, K.G.

lit.   C. E. C. Tattersall, *A History of British Carpets*, pp.100-101.

---

[1] William Cecil—Lord Burghley 1520-1598 (q.v.)

[2] Robert Cecil, 1st Earl of Salisbury and 1st Viscount Cranbourne, 1563-1612.

[3] De Farcy—*La Broderie*. 2nd Supplement. Angers. 1919. Plates CCLXXXII and CCXCIII.

[4] Victoria and Albert Museum, The Franco-British Exhibition of Textiles 1921. (H.M.S.O. 1922).

PLATE 6   ELIZABETHAN TABLE CARPET   *9ft. 9in. by 5ft. 6in.*

4th Quarter 16th Century—c. 1600 A.D.

BY COURTESY OF THE VICTORIA AND ALBERT MUSEUM

Another fine table carpet belonging to the Victoria and Albert Museum (No. T.125-1913), dating from about 1600, and worked entirely in tent-stitch in wool and some silk on a linen canvas. There are about 18 stitches to the inch, corresponding to 320 knots to the square inch in a pile carpet. In the middle there is a large panel with figures in Elizabethan dress at a Banquet. Also depicted, is a lady stabbing herself in the corner of the room. The space outside this panel is divided by broad strapwork into small sections of various shapes which contain landscapes, animals and plumed human heads. The whole is in natural colours somewhat faded. The identification of the subject of the centre panel presented some difficulty, for it was not realised at first that two separate incidents were included in one picture. The accidental discovery of a contemporary print showing the same scene proves beyond doubt that it represents the story of Lucrece!

ill.   Cyril G. E. Bunt, *Tudor and Stuart Fabrics*, Fig. 31.
lit.   C. E. C. Tattersall, *A History of British Carpets.* p.101-2.

PLATE 7   ELIZABETHAN TABLE CARPET   *13ft. by 5ft. 9in.*

4th Quarter 16th Century—c. 1600

BY COURTESY OF THE VICTORIA AND ALBERT MUSEUM

A well preserved table carpet, bought with the help of the National Art Collections Fund, and is in the Victoria and Albert Museum (No. T.134-1928). It is worked on a linen canvas entirely in polychrome silk tent-stitch. There are about 20 stitches to the square inch, equivalent to 400 knots to the inch in a pile carpet, of an exceedingly fine texture. The field has a white ground with a vine-covered trellis in natural colours. The wide border shows a landscape (twice repeated so that opposite sides and ends correspond) with figures of ladies and huntsmen, animals, houses, trees and flowers, each in their appropriate colours. The date is about 1600. There is no doubt that this was intended for use on a table. As is, unfortunately, so often the case with objects worked in tent-stitch, the carpet has got pulled very much out of shape. The difficulty of exhibiting it has been met by placing it on a table which is equally irregular!

col.   Formerly at Castle Bromwich Hall.
lit.   C. E. C. Tattersall, *A History of British Carpets*, p.101.
rep.   A. F. Kendrick, *English Decorative Fabric of the 16th to 18th Centuries*, Plate 19.
               Cyril G. E. Bunt, *Tudor & Stuart Fabrics*, Fig. 22.

PLATE 8   LATE 16th CENTURY TABLE CARPET   *10ft. 6in. by 5ft. 4in.*

4th Quarter 16th Century—c. 1600

BY COURTESY OF MR. C. F. J. BEAUSIRE

Probably English, but could well be French or Flemish, until more reliable data is obtained. This has been attributed to a probable English production because of its general composition, its leafage and scrolling and very unusual features. Similar to the Hulse carpet (Plate No. 12). Note too its great similarity to the Bolingbroke Carpet (Plate No. 10).

For instance in the border, an elephant and castle, a lion and unicorn, this being repeated in the central panel. They most probably are symbolic of medieval bestieries and were very prevalent in Elizabethan, Stuart and earlier embroideries. The arrangement of the trees is similar to embroideries which were later carried out in this country, for bed covers, valances, etc.

The border illustrates a farmhouse with ducks on a pond in one corner, a windmill with swans upon a lake (restored), in another. The fourth has a simple river with two swans. The remainder of the border has trees in fruit, and birds in variety, a leopard, a lion with its kill in its jaws, a unicorn and again an elephant and castle.

The centre, an all-over design of foliage with flowers and fruits, interspersed with birds and animals, includes a snake, and a narrow outer border with fringe. Worked in wool on canvas in fine petit point in blues, greens, fawns, yellows, etc. The whole in excellent condition.

col.   Arditti & Mayorcas, London.

PLATE 9   FRAGMENT OF TABLE CARPET   4ft. 10in. by 2ft. 8in.
1st Quarter 17th Century—c. 1600
BY COURTESY OF THE VICTORIA AND ALBERT MUSEUM

A fragment in the Victoria and Albert Museum's collection of fragments and documents of needlework (No. 7099-1860) worked in coloured wools and silks on linen canvas, in long-armed cross-stitch, cross-stitch and tent-stitch. Obviously part of a table cover.

Here again one cannot fail to notice the similarity in design, scrollings, birds, flowers etc., to the Hulse Carpet (Plate No. 12), the Bolingbroke Carpet (Plate No. 10) and the Beausire Carpet (Plate No. 8).

PLATE 10   ELIZABETHAN CARPET   13ft. 9in. by 6ft. 9in.
1st Quarter 17th Century—c. 1602
BY COURTESY OF THE VICTORIA AND ALBERT MUSEUM

Acquired with the aid of The National Art Collections Fund at the same time as 'The Gifford Carpet' and from the same collection Museum No. T.152-1930. It is worked in wool on linen canvas, mostly in tent-stitch, with the ground and part of the shields in long-armed tent-stitch. There are about 24 stitches to the inch, which is equivalent to the extremely fine texture of 576 knots to the inch in a pile carpet. The field has a blue ground with an all-over pattern of scrolling stems bearing flowers and fruit. It is very reminiscent of the design of The Hulse Carpet (Plate No. 12) and of the Heraldic Carpet at Knole.[1] The central medallion bearing the coat of arms, and embroidered in tent-stitch, on a dark green ground with a floral pattern similar to the general character of the field, but somewhat differently rendered, has in the scrolling alentours the initials J O on one side and E S on the other. On each side of the crest in the centre appears the initials O S and again E S. The border on a very dark green ground with a floral pattern similar to that of the field, has 16 Heraldic Shields arranged at regular intervals, each having a name embroidered above the shield. The border clearly shows that it has been sewn on and suggests that the carpet has been reduced in size at some time. The coats-of-arms commemorates the marriage of Oliver St. John, Earl of Bolingbroke, and Elizabeth Paulet, which took place in the year 1602.

col.   Lord St. John of Bletsoe.
lit.   C. E. C. Tattersall, *A History of British Carpets*, p.100.
repr.   Kendrick, Plate 18.

[1] Tattersall—*A History of British Carpets*. Plate No. 9.

PLATE 11   A TABLE CARPET
OF THE PERIOD OF JAMES I OF ENGLAND
1st Quarter 17th Century—c. 1610
BY COURTESY OF THE MARQUESS OF SALISBURY

A delightful table carpet of the first few years of the reign of James I of England, James VI of Scotland. It is worked in cross-stitch on canvas in coloured wools of natural colourings. The background of the central panel is embroidered in deep peacock-blue, with scrolling stems and foliage in green. The floral pattern with pink and red roses, China blue convolvulus has bunches of grapes and vine leaves in natural colours hanging on delicate graceful scrolling stems.

There appears to be a 'greyhound' or 'hare' in the bottom left hand corner, just above which there is a 'lizard' or 'tadpole', emerging to the right of a flower. Directly opposite this, on the other side of the field, stands a lion. From research, it has been conclusively proven that these animals have no armorial significance, so their intrusion in the pattern must be attributed to the general influence of the designs of the period, which often depicted heraldic beasts.

The border on a peacock-blue ground has a scrolling floral pattern of convolvulus and other flowers. On each side of the main border there is a guard border of gold and silver colouring worked in a geometrical motif.

This exceedingly fine example of cross-stitch, is very similar in character and design to the Hulse Carpet dated 1614 (See plate No. 12). Both field and borders lack the formality of the latter. The borders of the Hatfield example tend to be a proportionate reflection of the central design, a frequent practice in earlier examples, whereas the Hulse borders are of a distinctly different nature from the field. It is therefore because of this and its family history that this example has been dated before the Hulse carpet.

The making of this rug is attributed to members of the Cecil family, in whose possession it has always been. It is said to have originally belonged to Lord Burghley (1520-1598), but it is more reasonable to assume that it belonged to Robert Cecil, first Earl of Salisbury and First Viscount Cranbourne 1563-1612.

PLATE 12   THE HULSE CARPET
1st Quarter 17th Century—Dated 1614
BY COURTESY OF SIR WESTROW HULSE, BART.

A magnificent example of Turkey-type weave in hand-knotted Ghiordes knot.[1] It has 62 knots to the square inch, with a red tapestry woven wool selvedge. The apple-green ground has scrolling stems bearing roses, honeysuckle, irises, hyacinths, pansies, grapes, pomegranates, cucumbers, etc., as well as butterflies and caterpillars. The border is of a more formal floral pattern.

Although not a needlework carpet, it is included, because of its date and the design of the central field. There can be no doubt that its design is of Italian origin and that variations were employed in designing nearly all the table carpets of the first half of the 17th century that are illustrated. It is reasonable to assume that this type of design came to this country via Flanders. Its date too, gives a good guide to dating these other examples and for this reason it is an indispensable illustration.

exhib.   Victoria and Albert Museum, London (Loan exhibit).
lit.   C. E. C. Tattersall, *A History of British Carpets.* pp. 43 and 86. Illustrated Plate 7.

---

[1] Turki or Turkish Knot, to give it its correct nomenclature. Ghiordes being a little town in Western Anatolia.

PLATE 13 JAMES I TABLE CARPET 11ft. 1in. by 7ft. 1½in.
1st Quarter 17th Century—c. 1615
BY COURTESY OF THE CITY ART MUSEUM, ST. LOUIS, U.S.A.

An early 17th century table carpet (Museum No. 16-28) worked in cross-stitch and tent-stitch in coloured wools on a linen canvas. The prevailing colourings, dark green, browns, and blues; in the centre of the carpet a monogram B.D.G. impaled on a diagonal line on a blue ground. The design of this table is obviously Flemish inspired as are most of the table carpets of this period. This carpet has been dated early in the 17th century because its design in the central panel seems to be a development of the central panel of the Hulse carpet (see plate No. 12). The floral formation and large scrolling effect is more akin to the early part of the 17th century rather than the Elizabethan period.
Acquired by the Museum from the London Dealer, Mr. Cyril Andrade.

PLATE 14 TABLE CARPET FRAGMENT 13¾in. by 5¼in.
1st Quarter 17th Century—c. 1620
BY COURTESY OF THE VICTORIA AND ALBERT MUSEUM

Another fragment of the early 17th century, worked in coloured wools, silks and linens, in long-armed cross-stitch on linen canvas. (Museum No. T266-1934). Panel measures 13½in. by 5¼in.
coll. Victoria and Albert Museum, London—fragments and documents English Needlework.

PLATE 15 CHARLES I TABLE CARPET 9ft. 4in. by 6ft. 2in.
2nd Quarter 17th Century—c. 1630
BY COURTESY OF THE CITY OF BIRMINGHAM MUSEUM AND ART GALLERY

A needlework table carpet of the second quarter of the 17th century, slightly faded, but a most unusual design. It has geometrical medallions enclosing birds and beasts. The background worked in a design reminiscent of the Caucasian Rugs and akin to the designs employed at about this time on needlework carpets and rugs being produced in Portugal (Arraiolos).[1] It is worked in cross-stitch on canvas with passages of *petit point*. The whole enclosed with a Turkey work pattern border measuring 9½in. across.

PLATE 16 MID 17th CENTURY TABLE COVER 8ft. 4in. by 5ft. 4in.
2nd Quarter 17th Century—c. 1640
BY COURTESY OF MR. AND MRS. LONDON, PARIS

This is a superb example of a 17th century table cover. Worked in polychrome wools, of green, blue, yellow, brick, etc., in cross, tent and long-armed cross-stitches.
The design is a freely adapted interpretation of one of the many Italian designs flooding into North-West Europe for translating into tapestry at the looms of Brussels, Amsterdam or Mortlake. The scene, a completely disproportionate and undisciplined representation of trees, landscape, flowers, dwellings, birds and animals has a serenity, simplicity and unsophisticated charm seen

---

[1] See the large green 17th century Arraiolos carpet in the Museo Nacional de Arte Antiga—Lisbon.

once in High Gothic times, again here in the early 17th century and never repeated. The border (a strong similarity to the centre of the Hulse Carpet, Plate   ) has Italianate scrollings of leaves, flowers and grapes, with intertwining branches and stems. Each of the four corners contains a heraldic beast.

Clarity of design, definition and colour, together with the similarity of the border with that of the Hulse carpet, have induced me to ascribe an English origin to this panel, despite obvious temptations to associate it with Flanders. Since the source of design (Italy) is so often identical, the ascribing of a provenance to carpets at this time is often a very delicate matter.

PLATE 17   CHARLES II TABLE CARPET   10ft. 7in. by 7ft. 6in.

3rd Quarter 17th Century—Dated 1661

BY COURTESY OF MRS. J. M. PONTREMOLI, LONDON

Worked in tent-stitch and cross-stitch, in coloured silks, wools and metal threads on canvas, this very rare and interesting table carpet is reputed to have been made by a Royalist family for Charles II. Dated 1661 in silver metal threads, it bears the initials V.C.F.V.C.G.B.V.G.Z.D. also in silver metal thread. It was, it is felt, probably made as a celebration of the Restoration. It has a central oval medallion on a 'bleu-vert' ground with the figure of Justice, bandage removed, being given the heavenly crown of wisdom. Around her, again on a blue-vert ground, is a scattering of flowers, fruit and birds in naturalistic colours, in great detail: for instance below and above her is a pared lemon, still with its rind in one piece. This in turn is enclosed by eight tasselled silk swags, hung with grapes, melons and pomegranates and joined with four evenly spaced fruit laden baskets. All in shades of apricot, blues, pinks, yellows, etc.

In the four corners are the figures of Faith (Crucifix), Hope (Dove and Anchor), Charity (Heart beaten on an anvil) and Fecundity (Babies). The continual reference to Fecundity in this charming table carpet, together with its symbols of pomegranates, fig-trees, grapes, etc., may well refer to the King's contemplated marriage to Catherine of Braganza in 1662.

The border on a pistache colour ground has a scrolling pattern of stylized flowers, carnations, peonies, roses, lillies, tulips in natural colours reminiscent in style and manner of the Indian embroideries.

Obviously a table carpet because of its concentric design, this is a good example of the designs employed in the earlier half of the 17th century, such as the stylized floral border akin to stomachers and embroidered panels of the time of Charles I. The scattered flowers and fruits too can be seen in fine petit point embroidered pictures of this period. Understandably after the Commonwealth (1648-1659) design had not yet entered into its own, hence the similarity with designs of the pre Cromwellian period.

The inscription and date cannot unfortunately be clearly seen on this plate, because they are worked in silver metal thread.

PLATE 18   TURKEY WORK CARPET   11ft. 5in. by 7ft. 8in.

3rd Quarter 17th Century—Dated 1672

BY COURTESY OF THE VICTORIA AND ALBERT MUSEUM

A Turkey work pile carpet, hand knotted in coloured wools at 55 knots to the square inch. Has a plain web selvedge. Its colours, black field with an all-over mass of closely packed flowers and leaves. In the middle a shield with the arms of Molyneux impaling Rigby. Sir John Molyneux of

Teversall (1625-1691) having married Lucy daughter of Alexander Rigby, Esqre., of Middleton. It bears the 'bloody hand' of Ulster—the badge of a baronet—it is rather amusing to note that Sir John became a baronet in 1674.

This fine example bears a strong resemblance to the Turkey work that developed later in the century. It has been included for reference to show the development of the pile carpet and the decline of the canvas work carpet in the second half of the 17th century. No doubt, fashion, changing decor, and demand, brought about the wane of needlework carpets in this period.

lit. C. E. C. Tattersall, *A History of British Carpets, plate 10*, pp. 48 and 87.

PLATE 19   QUEEN ANNE CARPET   8ft. 5in. by 5ft. 4½in.

1st Quarter 18th Century—c. 1705

BY COURTESY OF MESSRS. PHILLIPS OF HITCHIN, LTD.

This rather interesting design with classical scenes is in the style of the famous needlework hangings from Stoke Edith, now at Montacute in Somerset. In this carpet *Zeus* is shown beneath the parrot sitting on his throne with his thunderbolts in his left hand. In the clouds above the tree is *Juno* in a chariot drawn by her two peacocks. On the left of Zeus is the winged *Hermes*, and on the right *Artemis* with her bow. Beneath them on the right is *Athene* with her Medusa shield, and *Ares* with bow and quiver of arrows. The depiction of these Gods and Goddesses in 18th century costume is amusing, and the colours too are delightfully fresh. This carpet has been dated as circa 1705 as the influence is very Dutch. The central panel is very reminiscent of fine tent-stitch needlework which was being made in Delft and Leyden in Holland in the late 1680's and sometimes erroneously referred to in this country as being English. The outside border still retains the strong influence of Jacobean crewel work with an introduction to the design which is more apparent in the examples of about 1710.

coll. Lord Ivor Spencer Churchill.
    Arditti & Mayorcas, London.
    S. W. Wolsey, London.

PLATE 20   QUEEN ANNE CARPET   Approx. 7ft. 6in. by 5ft. 5in.

1st Quarter 18th Century—c. 1710

PRESENT OWNERSHIP UNKNOWN

An early 18th century example of the Queen Anne period. In fine condition with remarkably fresh colours. Worked in cross-stitch in polychrome silks on three linen canvas widths. The ground of a Chinese lacquer red with the design in yellows, blues, greens, etc.

coll. Arditti & Mayorcas, London (1957).
    Ginsburg & Levy, New York.

PLATE 21 (top)   QUEEN ANNE CARPET   7ft. 11in. by 7ft. 9in.
                          1st Quarter 18th Century—c. 1710
                          PRESENT OWNERSHIP UNKNOWN

Eighteenth century needlework of circa 1710 worked with huge multi-coloured stems and curling
leafage, bearing heads of various garden flowers. Worked in polychrome wools on linen canvas
in tent-stitch. The floral design mounted on a larger panel of canvas, worked in, and the ground
filled in with cross-stitch of brown wool. This brown field was worked in at a much, much later
date. Although the carpet is not as it was originally, it has been included simply to show the continuity of design at about this time.

auct.   Parke-Bernet Galleries Inc, New York.
               14th-15th March, 1958, Lot 366
               Clearly stated—brown field—re-appliqué—with 18th century needlepoint (needlework).

PLATE 21 (bottom)   GEORGE I CARPET   6ft. by 4ft. 6in.
                          1st Quarter 18th Century—c. 1720
                          BY COURTESY OF MRS. DAVID GUBBAY

From the collection of Mrs. David Gubbay we illustrate this 'exotic' needlework carpet. Worked
in tent-stitch and cross-stitch in many coloured wools, on canvas strips, it has a field of green
covered by a mass of large 'exotic' blooms, carnations, peonies, chrysanthemums in shades of
reds and blues with large stylized leaves and other flowers. The whole is enclosed within a small
diaper pattern border in alternating colours of light and dark red and blue.
This carpet shows the large blooms from the turn of the century and at the same time shows the
free, imaginative and unbalanced designs of the baroque-rococo 'transition' period. It still retains
the Indian 'Jacobean' stylization we got to know so well in the latter half of the 17th century but
has a certain charm and grace of movement so well developed by the English craftsmen of the
early part of the 18th century.

PLATE 22   GEORGIAN CARPET   approx. 9ft. by 7ft.
                          1st Quarter 18th Century—c. 1725
                      BY COURTESY OF MESSRS. ROFFÉ & RAPHAEL
                          THE VIGO ART GALLERIES, LONDON

An early 18th century floral carpet where one can clearly see the continuation, trend and development from heavy 'Jacobeanish' design. (See plates 19, 20, 21.) A very pleasing arrangement worked
in polychrome wools, in cross-stitch, on a linen canvas—two widths employed. The foliage in
shades of deep green, the flowers in natural colours on a soft yellow ground. An effective double
border encloses the floral centre.

PLATE 23   GEORGE II CARPET   10ft. 7in. by 8ft. 6in.
                            2nd Quarter 18th Century—dated 1730
                          BY COURTESY OF MRS. DAVID GUBBAY

At Trent Park, Mrs. Gubbay has amongst her well known collection of antiques and works of art,
this very informative needlework carpet. It is worked in polychrome wools in cross-stitch on
canvas, the central polygonal medallion suggestive of the Indian form on a fawn colour ground,
is worked with flowers in various colours around a giant sunflower. The field of brown and blue
is covered with a mass of stylized flowers in red, yellow, pink, fawn and green foliage and clearly
shows the early influence of the rococo. From each corner emerges a spray of carnations, irises,
lillies, etc., in naturalistic colours tied in bows with ribbons.
This carpet is most unusual in that it has two main borders, one floral and the other geometrical.
The floral border of tulips, daffodils, daisies has a giant sunflower in each corner to repeat and
balance the sunflower in the central medallion. Inside the floral border, the guard border of lozenges
and diaper forms and on the outside a 'water-leaf' guard.
The outer border has alternate libate motifs and lozenges which repeat every sixth time. The field
of this unusual border also has a scattering of carnations and other flowers in variegated colours.
This carpet is most interesting because of its date—see the detail section. It clearly shows how the
rococo began to infiltrate the floral designs of this period. It shows too the Indian influence in its
medallion (probably taken from Palampores of this period). The outside border is a curious mixture
of formality and assymetry.

PLATE 24   GEORGE II VASE CARPET   10ft. 9in. by 8ft. 6in.
                            2nd Quarter 18th Century—c. 1730
                    BY COURTESY OF JUDGE IRWIN UNTERMYER, NEW YORK

This is a 'Vase Carpet' on canvas worked in coloured wools, using tent-stitch, brick-stitch and gros-
point. The colouring in shades of green, yellow, beige, pink, red, blue and grey. Sold in 1933, and
according to the information in the sale catalogue: 'This carpet was worked by the Misses Rowland
great-great aunts of the present owner (Miss M. E. Redgate), circa 1730'. A carpet, apparently very
similar, is described in the catalogue of a sale of the contents of Strawberry Hill (1842) as 'A needlework carpet, black ground, richly worked with flowers, 3¾ yards by 3 yards, on the sixteenth
day's sale, lot 36'.

coll.   Miss M. E. Redgate.
auct.   Sotheby's. 15th December 1933. (Lot 185)
illus.   Dr. Hackenbroch, *English and Other Needlework, Tapestries and Textiles in the Irwin
               Untermyer Collection.* Figure 143. Plate 105. (New York. 1960).

PLATE 25   THE RABY CARPET   26ft. by 16ft.
                            2nd Quarter 18th Century—c. 1730
                          BY COURTESY OF LORD BARNARD

This large carpet, belonging to The Lord Barnard, is worked in polychrome wools on a linen canvas
entirely in cross-stitch. There are five stitches to the inch, equivalent to 25 knots to the inch in a
pile carpet. It is therefore of somewhat coarse texture. The colourings are mainly yellow, blue
and pink, with the fret-pattern border in yellow or red.

The edges have been cut, apparently in one instance, to make room for a fireplace. The Duchess of Cleveland, writing in 1870 says, 'The carpet was the work of The Lady Grace Fitzroy, Countess of Darlington, and must therefore be about 140 years old. At one time it was kept jealously rolled up and never used, but it has not been taken much care of since'. The Lady Grace Fitzroy, who was the beautiful Barbara Villiers, granddaughter of Charles II, married in 1725, Henry, Third Baron Bernard and First Earl of Darlington.

The design of this carpet is very much in the neo-classical of the Kent and Burlington School. At first sight one might have strong doubts about the authenticity of the Duchess of Cleveland's claims. Unfortunately anything classical in design of the 18th century—erroneously—is automatically associated with the Adam Brothers, and therefore is said to belong to the second half of the century. There is nevertheless, a distinct difference of mood and style between the design of this carpet and the later designs used by Robert Adam for his tufted pile carpets at Moorfields.

The Raby carpet has none of the severe elegance of Adam neo-classicism but rather a vivacity and flow associated with the rococo influences of the first half of the century. It seems however, quite obvious that the designer was entirely unaware of this intrusion into what he undoubtedly believed to be a contemporary interpretation of classical design.

repr.   C. E. C. Tattersall, *A History of British Carpets*, Pl. 28.
exhib.   Bowes Museum, Barnard Castle, Yorkshire (on loan)

PLATES 26 & 27   EARLY GEORGIAN CARPET   10ft. 2in. by 7ft.
                         2nd Quarter 18th Century—c. 1735
                    BY COURTESY OF COLONEL WILLIAMSBURG, VIRGINIA, U.S.A.

Worked in polychrome wools on linen canvas in tent-stitch. There are about 9 to 10 stitches to the inch which is equivalent to 90 knots to the square inch in a pile carpet. The field has a pattern of knarled vine-stems on a yellow ground. In the middle, a panel on a dark green ground, contains a basket of flowers within a shield edged with heavy gadroons. The luxuriance and exuberance of the stems in the wide border, with their variety of blossoms, recalls the hangings adapted from Indian Palampores.

We show both the carpet as a whole (Plate 26) and also in its present setting in restored Williamsburg. (Plate 27).

coll.   Sir Charles Welby, Bart.
exhib.   Victoria and Albert Museum, London (on loan).
repr.   A. F. Kendrick, *English Decorative Fabrics of the 16th to 18th Centuries*, Pl. 49.
             C. E. C. Tattersall, *A History of British Carpets*, Pl. 26.

PLATE 28   GEORGE II CARPET   8ft. by 8ft.
                         2nd Quarter 18th Century—c. 1735
                       BY COURTESY OF MRS. DAVID GUBBAY

This exceptional carpet is worked in polychrome wools in cross-stitch on canvas, has a central 'lozenge' medallion, containing a large, stylized sunflower. The rest of the field is devoted to the conventional mass of semi-exotic multi-coloured flowers and foliage in red, yellow, white and greens. The design in this case flows outwards from the centre, rather than inwards from the corners. The main border, inside two guards consists of formal scrollings and stylized foliage in blue-green with a peony and sunflower in natural colours in diagonally opposite corners. The outer guard on a yellow ground has a scrolling oak leaf pattern in red, and the inner guard an alternating scroll and quatrefoil in yellow and red on a blue ground with an oak leaf in each corner. A curious feature of this carpet is that the selvedge has an insertion of the original wool colour samples that were used in the working. The canvas, showing, was worn, evidence of stencilling, or it may even have been the painting or drawing of the design.

coll.   Arditti & Mayorcas, London.
          Frank Partridge & Sons, Ltd., London.

PLATE 29   GEORGIAN RUG   9ft. by 6ft. 6in.
                    2nd Quarter 18th Century—c. 1735
                BY COURTESY OF THE HERITAGE FOUNDATION
             AND LOCATED AT DEERFIELD, MASSACHUSSETTS, U.S.A.

At Deerfield, Mass. U.S.A., there is this most interesting needlework rug, worked in polychrome wools, in cross-stitch on canvas. The field of the centre and border, a royal blue, except on one side, where restoration and fading has created a lightish green shade. The central field is scattered with various floral sprays, including tulips, peonies, carnations and exotic birds in flight. Fresh colours of yellows, reds, greens, blues and lavenders are generally employed.
The trailing floral border with similar flowers in swags and tied with bows emerge from cornucopia at each corner. The guard stripe on each side of the main border is beige darkening to rust brown.
The grace and movement of the floral border is suggestive of the surrounds seen on Flemish Verdure tapestries of the middle of the 17th century. The central panel, with its scattered floral sprays and its exotic birds in flight (Phoenix) points to a Chinoiserie rendering of the Delft Tulip Tapestries of the late 17th century. Examples of such tapestries can be seen at the Delft Museum, and at the Boymans Museum at Rotterdam.
[1]In design, layout and definition, the central field can be compared with an embroidered muslin apron in the Cooper Union Collection, New York, U.S.A. This muslin apron is signed S.K. and dated 1733.
Unfortunately there is no known history to this exceedingly interesting example, which is exhibited at the Wright House of the Heritage Foundation located at Deerfield, Mass., U.S.A.

coll.   Messrs. Ginsburg and Levy, New York, U.S.A.

PLATE 30   GEORGE II CARPET   approx. 10ft. by 8ft.
                    2nd Quarter 18th Century.—c. 1740
                BY COURTESY OF SIR HUBERT MEDLYCOTT, BART

This carpet of about 1740 is in similar style to that of the Holt carpet (Plate 38) (now in the Metropolitan Museum of Art) although the design is simpler and more sparse. It will be observed that some of the stems on the example are tied in bunches with ribbons. Although both these carpets are well in line with English design and style of the period, there is a distinct Oriental influence

---

[1] See the Chronicle of the Museum for the Arts of Decoration for the Cooper Union Museum, Vol. 2. No. 7. June 1955. Fig. 18, page 220.

about them. The curved motif in the centre of Untermyer's carpet, with a segment of a similar motif in each corner, is the most popular of all Oriental carpet designs. It is probable that the designers of these two carpets were quite unaware of the Oriental basis of their pattern, since the influence was probably derived from intermediate sources. One very likely source was the tremendously popular imports of printed and painted cottons and linens from India ('Indiennes' and 'pintados'), whose designs most probably had an influence, consciously or unconsciously, on textile designers in England.

illus. A. F. Kendrick, *English Decorative Fabrics of the 16th to 18th Centuries, 1934*, Plate 48.
exhib. V. and A. Museum, London, 1921.

PLATE 31 EARLY GEORGIAN CARPET 7ft. 3in. by 4ft. 6in.
2nd Quarter 18th Century—c. 1740
BY COURTESY OF THE TRUSTEES OF THE LADY LEVER ART GALLERY
PORT SUNLIGHT, CHESHIRE
MUSEUM NO. X2566

An unusual design, it could perhaps be described as a reflection of the time, with its 18th century costumed figures, its peacocks, parrots and birds in variety. A novel feature is that each of the four corners has a mermaid. The unusual note is the centre piece of formalized flowerheads, with two vases of flowers adjacent. This kind of design, together with birds and parrots in concentric form seem to have been popular on embroidered covers of Castelo Branco (Nr. Lisbon, Portugal) and on Arraiolos table carpets of the first half of the 18th century. It could well be that after further research this carpet will be attributed to Arraiolos provenance.

The whole is helped by its very pleasing colour. The centre ground of greenish drab with areas of faded pink: the motifs in light blue, pink and yellowish drab outlined in chocolate brown with some yellow. The outer border composed entirely of birds on a chocolate brown ground.

PLATES 32 and 33 GEORGE II CARPET 9ft. 6in. by 5ft. 4in.
2nd Quarter 18th Century—c. 1740
BY COURTESY OF THE TRYON PALACE, NEW BERN, NORTH CAROLINA, U.S.A.

A fine example of the English needlework carpets made around the 1740's, worked in polychrome colours in wool, on two widths of linen canvas. The whole in varying shades of rose red, blue, green and yellow on a brown ground, worked in long- and short-stitch. The embroidery, somewhat similar to crewel work, but with no canvas showing.

The Tryon Palace was originally built under the supervision of the English Architect John Hawks, who commenced it in the year 1767 and was completed in 1770. It served not only as the 'Capitol', but also as the Governor's residence. The Royal Governor was William Tryon 1767-1770. The main building was destroyed by fire in 1798, and it was not until 1952 that its complete restoration was begun. It is today described as the most beautiful building in the Colonial Americas. The interior rooms are furnished throughout, as near as possible to the original—the drawing room is listed as one of the one hundred finest rooms in America. The library contains the original editions of books owned by Governor William Tryon. In addition to illustrating this needlework carpet (Plate 32), it is shown in its setting (Plate 33). This illustration shows the upstairs supper room with its 18th century furnishing, and the carpet with its design of three large upstanding poppy plants in bloom.

coll. Ohan Berberyan, New York.

40

PLATE 34 HATFIELD HOUSE CARPET 9ft. by 6ft.

2nd Quarter 18th Century—c. 1740

BY COURTESY OF THE MARQUESS OF SALISBURY

This exquisite and perhaps the finest example of 18th century wool embroidery on canvas that exists is in the possession of The Marquess of Salisbury, at Hatfield House, Hitchin, Herts. It is worked in fine coloured wools and silks on canvas, entirely in tent-stitch, with a few details emphasised with French knots. Closely packed flowers and leaves in natural fresh colours, worked on an almost black ground covers the entire centre of this carpet. The natural fresh coloured flowers in profusion are repeated in the border, but on a coral ground. Embroidered on each side of the main border there is a simple ribbon-pattern stripe, which enhances the whole.
In a very good state of preservation.

illus.   Mrs. Guy Antrobus and Louisa Preece, *Needlework through the Ages*, 1928. Pl. 85.
C. E. C. Tattersall, *A History of British Carpets*, 1934, frontispiece.

PLATE 35   GEORGE II TABLE CARPET   12ft. 11in. by 9ft. 4in.

2nd Quarter 18th Century—c. 1740

BY COURTESY OF THE LORD FAIRHAVEN

A rare early 18th century table carpet, worked in coloured wools, on four widths of canvas in cross-stitch. The centre panel depicts a landscape scene. Enclosed by a wall with red doors is a group of brick houses with blue roofs, on the bank of a river. In the foreground, on the branches of trees with thickly clustered leaves, are perched exotic birds, in reds, blues and browns. Beneath, amongst the hillocks there are red and gold flowers. The whole is on a snuff coloured ground, within a four-sided border of roses, tulips, carnations and other summer flowers in fresh natural colours. Edging each side of the border are red and white poles entwined with oak leaves. The cartouches in the four corners are worked with the arms of the Kirkcaldy and Sheldon families.
The colourings are very fresh.

coll.   The late Viscount Leverhulme.
Messrs. Arditti & Mayorcas, London.
illus.   Catalogue of the Art Collection of the late Viscount Leverhulme. Plate No. 25.
Anderson Galleries, New York, 1926.

PLATE 36   GEORGE II CARPET   10ft. by 7ft.

2nd Quarter 18th Century—c. 1740

BY COURTESY OF THE TRUSTEES OF THE LADY LEVER ART GALLERY
PORT SUNLIGHT, CHESHIRE

Port Sunlight have three examples, this is the second to be noted (Museum No. X. 4063); an all-over floral and leaf design with a central medallion and double border. The centre field in dark blue with the floral and foliate motifs in red, yellow, green, blue and drab. The outer border on a scarlet ground, with the motifs in blue, yellow and green. The whole embroidered on four widths of canvas in polychrome wools, in cross-stitch.

PLATE 37   GEORGE II CARPET   8ft. 3in. by 7ft. 6in.
                              2nd Quarter 18th Century—c. 1740
                    BY COURTESY OF COLONEL WILLIAMSBURG, VIRGINIA, U.S.A.

This example is worked in polychrome wools in cross-stitch. The brown field with central lozenge-shaped floral motif and four triangular spandrel-form floral sprays, each arranged in a cornucopia. The inner and outer guards in biege strapwork design frame the floral-patterned brown ground border. Flowers include tulips, lilies, roses, carnations, daffodils, morning glories and chrysanthemums. Shaded brilliantly in red, blue, yellow and white, with green leaves.

exhib.   British Antique Dealer's Fair, Grosvenor House, London, 1958.
              Art Treasures Exhibition, Bath, May 29th to June 29th, 1958.
              (illustrated in catalogue. Plate 69).
repr.   *Apollo Magazine*, May, 1958.
coll.   Arditti & Mayorcas, London.

PLATE 38   GEORGE II CARPET   11ft. by 5ft. 6in.
                        2nd Quarter 18th Century—signed and dated 1743
                    BY COURTESY OF THE METROPOLITAN MUSEUM OF ART, NEW YORK

Embroidered in cross-stitch with coloured wools on a linen canvas. It has about 8 or 9 stitches to the inch, which corresponds to about 75 knots to the square inch in a pile carpet. The field has a lobed diamond shaped panel in the middle and four corner pieces. This arrangement was very common in Oriental designs. Fields, border and panels are filled with closely packed blossoms in natural colours. At one end are the initials 'E.N.' and the date 1743. In the central medallion and corner motifs we once again see the strong influence of the Indian painted and printed cottons and linens (Pintados and Indiennes) popular at this time. At one period belonging to the late Mr. W. J. Holt, it was acquired by Judge Irwin Untermyer. Placed on loan at the Metropolitan Museum since 1958, it was finally presented to them by the Judge in 1962.
Museum No. 62.1.

coll.   W. J. Holt.
              Judge Irwin Untermyer.
illus.   A. F. Kendrick, *English Decorative Fabrics of the 16th to the 18th Centuries*, 1934. Plate 47.
              C. E. C. Tattersall, *A History of British Carpets*, 1934. Plate 27.
exhib.   Loan Exhibition of English Decorative Art, at Lansdowne House, 1929. No. 349.
              Plate 72.
              New York Art Treasures of the 18th century, Parke Bernet Galleries Inc. 1942. No. 577

PLATE 39   GEORGE II CARPET   7ft. 8½in. by 7ft. 4in.
                        2nd Quarter 18th Century—Signed and dated 1743.
                    BY COURTESY OF JUDGE IRWIN UNTERMYER, NEW YORK, U.S.A.

This signed and dated carpet is an extremely informative example. It is the only one that I have been able to trace which shows clearly the anglicised version of the rocaille. Rocaille was a decorative art originating in France around 1700. Rampant at the time of Louis XV it was transported over here to replace the Baroque and eventually triumph in about 1754. The rococo assymetry is recognised by 'C' scrolls. Hence the border and the field around the medallion is in this new form of decor, whilst the central vase and floral motif retains the earlier baroque designs. It is signed H.T. and dated 6 Oct. 1743. Worked in coloured wools in cross-stitch on canvas, it has a large fluted vase of flowers taking up the large central medallion. The decoratively arranged corner motifs are in the rococo arrangement of flower and leaf forms on a brown ground. The border is in a similar rococo traetment of flowers and leaves, in shades of beige, yellow, brown, pink, red, green and blue on a red ground with the 'C' scrolls interconnecting.

illus.   Dr. Hackenbroch, *English and other Needlework Tapestries and Textiles in the Irwin Untermyer Collection*, 1960. Fig. 144, Plate 106.

exhib.   New York, Art Treasures of the 18th century, Parke-Bernet Galleries Inc. 1942, No. 581.

PLATE 40   THE 'HOLTE' CARPET—GEORGE II   15ft. by 9ft. 6in.
                          2nd Quarter 18th Century—c. 1744
                 BY COURTESY OF THE CITY OF BIRMINGHAM MUSEUM AND ART GALLERY

Worked on rather a coarse canvas in cross-stitch, with tent-stitch in places, in polychrome wools, seven stitches to the inch. It is a very interesting carpet as we have seen.[1] The field richly embroidered with flowers and leaf design slightly suggestive again of the rococo—the eternal 'C'—in rose reds, blues, greens, and gold on a dark blue ground, in very fresh colourings. In the centre are the arms of the Holte family, and the whole is completed with floral and foliated borders in similar fresh colours. Inset at each corner a fluted motif in shaped medallions.

This carpet, worked by Mary Holte, around the year 1744, appears to be contemporary with a set of hangings in Aston Hall, Birmingham, which bears the inscription:

> 'God be my guide
> And the work will abide,
> Mary Holte, spinster aged 60, 1744'

On the back of the carpet is a label in a later hand stating 'This carpet was worked by Mary daughter of Sir Clobery Holte of Aston Hall, Birmingham, about 1744 and was intended for Charles the First's bedroom at Aston'. The carpet passed into the possession of Mary Elizabeth Holte, daughter of the last Baronet, who married Abraham Bracebridge, thence by family descent in the Brace-bridge and Compton-Bracebridge families, until finally its purchase by the City Museum and Art Gallery, Birmingham, about six years ago, ensured its availability for study.

lit.   *A History of the Holte's of Aston*, by Alfred Davidson, 1854, mentions and describes this carpet.

PLATE 41   GEORGE II CARPET   14ft. 6in. by 12ft. 8in.
                          3rd Quarter 18th Century—c. 1750
                 BY COURTESY OF MESSRS. FRANK PARTRIDGE & SONS LTD., LONDON

This very fine and beautiful example is reproduced in colour, and came from Eaton Hall, Chester, the family seat of the Duke of Westminster. The reddish brown field is centred by a diamond-shaped panel containing a bouquet of flowers and leaves. In shades of blue, pink, gold and cream, with a gold and cream edged border. The rest of the field is covered with a charmingly natural scroll-work of flowers and leaves, dahlias, roses, sunflowers and convolvulus in shades of blue,

---

[1]See p. 12.

pink, gold and cream. The wide outer border is similarly decorated, and is enclosed between two narrow cream stripes with a stylised leaf motif.

This carpet has a particularly interesting composition, as it makes a definite break with the Baroque and yet is without the elegant sophistication which the prime rococo contributions possessed. The concept of the design actually hankers somewhere between the two, and can be put into a classification of 'Transitional' carpets, that is to say between Baroque and Rococo.

coll.   The Duke of Westminster.
illus.   *Connoisseur* (June 1960)

PLATE 42   GEORGIAN CARPET   6ft. 7in. by 4ft. 10in.
3rd Quarter 18th Century—c. 1755
BY COURTESY OF MR. BENSON FORD, MICHIGAN, U.S.A.

A fine example of English needlework. A resurgence of the Indian design can be clearly seen in the treatment of the central medallion and corner motifs. The leaves around the medallion and corner motifs are very rococo in character, which of course helps to give a date to this rug. The sprays of blooms in each corner are particularly attractive and are tied with bows, the edging on all the medallions indicates a further strong rococo influence. A very elegant composition which would flatter any type of 18th century English decor.

coll.   Messrs. Phillips of Hitchin Ltd.
           Ohan Berberyan, New York.

PLATE 43   GEORGE II CARPET   10ft. 5in. by 8ft. 9in.
3rd Quarter 18th Century—c. 1755
BY COURTESY OF V. H. JINISHIAN, NEW YORK

This example is worked in cross-stitch, on a tobacco-brown ground. The central medallion, and its quarter-segments in each corner, are on a soft red field. The flowers both in and surrounding the medallion are in pastel hues of beige, gold, blue and green, together with touches of rose. There is a wide border, on each side of which is a narrow 'guard' border. Here again, the colourings and flowers follow the same pattern as the centre.

It is interesting to note the conglomeration of influences on the design. The obvious, exotic-Indian spread of flowers and foliage, the still-lingering Jacobean leaf, the Persian carpet principle of a medallion in the middle and segments of it in each corner and a strange Chinese feel about the thing as a whole.

PLATE 44   PAIR GEORGE III RUGS   each 4ft. 6in. by 2ft. 1in.
3rd Quarter 18th Century—c. 1760
IN THE POSSESSION OF MESSRS. ARDITTI AND MAYORCAS, LONDON

A pair of mid-18th century small rugs. The floral design indicates a Chinese influence. The colourings are pleasing; a field of terra-cotta with the floral arrangements in reds, blues, green and ivory. It is highly probable that these were made for window seats or alcoves. The rugs which are quite original, are worked in polychrome wools in cross-stitch on linen canvas. The whole enclosed by an embroidered galloon in string colour.

coll.   Arditti and Mayorcas, London.

PLATE 45   GEORGIAN CARPET   7ft. by 5ft. 6in.

3rd Quarter 18th Century—c. 1760

BY COURTESY OF COLONEL WILLIAMSBURG, VIRGINIA, U.S.A.

Embroidered in cross-stitch on linen canvas in polychrome wools. The central panel in a deep mazarine blue contains a circular medallion, outlined by a chain pattern in red. Within this, a design of tulips, roses, peonies, carnations, etc., in a stylised manner to give a chinoiserie effect. The four matching quarter medallions at the corners, again with a cluster of stylised flowers, are enclosed within a chain pattern border in red. (Note the central motif—similar to the Canton rose). The field has trailing stems of tulips, peonies, roses, etc. The old gold border with variegated leaf motifs in shaded blues, and touches of crimson with other colours. The main border outlined on each side by a chain stripe in blue. The whole is well preserved, in good rich colours and portrays the Chinese taste very prevalent in the third quarter of the 18th century.

illus.   Catalogue of a sale of antique and other fine rugs at The Parke-Bernet Galleries Inc., New York, November 19th, 1959. Item No. 19.

coll.   Edwina Countess Mountbatten of Burma.
S.W. Wolsey, London.
Frank Partridge and Sons Ltd., London.
Ohan Berberyan, New York, U.S.A.

PLATES 46 and 47   GEORGIAN CARPET   approximately 19ft. by 12ft.

3rd Quaretr 18th Century—c. 1760

BY COURTESY OF THE TRUSTEES OF HARVARD UNIVERSITY, U.S.A.

Typical of decoration towards the end of the rococo in this country. Worked in polychrome wools in cross-stitch at 36 stitches to the square inch, this is a very fine example indeed. The field entirely covered with rope-shaped lozenges contains an elongated floral medallion—mass of various flower—in natural colours complemented by quarter medallions in the corners with similar tulips, sunflowers, peonies, etc. The whole enclosed by a strong rococo border of variegated leaf forms and finished by a striped edging. The carpet is illustrated as it was in 1925 (Plate 46) and again after the repairs were completed at the Royal School of Needlework in 1954 (Plate 47). It has been backed by The Royal School of Needlework with a very fine scrim.

This carpet was acquired in London in 1925 by Mr. and Mrs. Robert Woods Bliss for their home Dumbarton Oaks. Dumbarton Oaks with its entire furnishings was given by Mr. and Mrs. Robert Woods Bliss to Harvard University.

N.B. There is in the collection of Mrs. David Gubbay a very similar carpet, a further pointer to professionalism seeing the similarity of layout of the borders and the central motif. The variation of the background can be accounted for too.

coll.   C. H. F. Kinderman-Walker, London, 1925.
Mr. and Mrs. Robert Woods Bliss.

PLATE 48   GEORGE III CARPET   9ft. 9in. by 8ft. 10in.
                            3rd Quarter 18th Century—signed and dated 1765
                          BY COURTESY OF THE METROPOLITAN MUSEUM OF ART, NEW YORK

An exceedingly brilliant coloured carpet worked on canvas in polychrome wools in reds, blues,
greens, etc. An all-over floral pattern —in the centre a rococo medallion. A very pretty and
symmetrical design. The date and initials AL JPI? 1765 can be seen in the lower left hand corner.
This carpet clearly portrays the beginning of the end of the rococo in this country in decor and
furnishings, although it continued for a much longer period in silver and porcelain. The waning
influence of the rococo is clearly discernible. It is worked in cross-stitch on linen canvas and was
acquired by The Metropolitan Museum of Art, New York, with the help of the Joseph Pillitzer
Bequest.

illus.   Met. Mus. Bulletin Vol. 29, 1934, *An English embroidered Carpet* pp. 60-62. The identi-
            fication of the maker and the provenance given in this article are no longer considered
            to be accurate.
            Preston Remington, *English Domestic Needlework*, Met. Mus., New York, 1945,
            Plate 41.

PLATE 49   GEORGE III CARPET   10ft. by 8ft. 6in.
                               3rd Quarter 18th Century—c. 1765
                              BY COURTESY OF V. H. JINISHIAN, NEW YORK

This carpet is worked in cross-stitch, with a dominating scalloped floral medallion on a maroon
ground. The flowers enclosed therein are in shades of yellow, blue, green, beige and red. Surrounding the medallion is a field of lobate trellis design, containing a four petal lobate flower on a green
ground. The four corner motifs each contain a single-flower spray. The wide border is on a vivid
yellow ground, with scrolls and foliage in blues, browns, green and beige. The narrow outer
border is the conventional Greek 'key' pattern border, with a single flower-face in each corner.
This border is in soft purply-blue, yellow and mauve.
The design of the carpet puts it clearly in the 'Transitional' stage, with the Rocaille influence losing
its hold to the Classical, albeit reluctantly, hence the very 'scrolly' border.

PLATE 50   'CHINOISERIE' CARPET   8ft. by 6ft. 4in.
                               3rd Quarter 18th Century—c. 1765
                              BY COURTESY OF MRS. DAVID GUBBAY

An example of the third quarter of the 18th century is this fine needlework carpet. It is
worked in tent-stitch and cross-stitch in fresh natural colours on a blue ground.
The field of blue has an all-over pattern of scattered quatre foil motifs with a round floral medallion
in the centre and enclosed by an arrowhead pattern. The central motif contains a mass of carnations,
tulips, peonies and other exotic blooms in natural colours together with foliage and worked in a
concentric design around a giant central sunflower in shades of red, blue and yellow.
Each corner contains a quarter segment of the central medallion, with flowers and enclosed within
again an arrowhead pattern frame. This lay-out is an adaption from 'Eastern' carpet designs.

The border also on a blue ground and contained within two narrow arrowhead guards has a trailing floral pattern of similar composition to the central medallion. Symmetry is maintained by a sunflower in each opposite corner and a peony in the other.

This carpet is typical of its period for it shows clearly the 'Chinoiserie' influence, the trend towards Classical simplicity with its scattered quatrefoil and the restoring of balance after the spate of rococo assymetry.

PLATE 51   **GEORGE III CARPET**   7ft. by 5ft. 9½in.

3rd Quarter 18th Century—c. 1770

BY COURTESY OF CAPTAIN R. F. EYRE HUDDLESTON, R.N. AND MRS. EYRE HUDDLESTON

This carpet, an 18th century example, clearly shows the beginning of the classical influence. It can be seen at Sawston Hall, near Cambridge, an historical house of great interest. It is worked in coloured wools in cross-stitch throughout. It has a diamond-shaped central medallion with a floral centre outlined with geometrically patterned leaves. Enclosed in a colourful frame, a larger inner border of flowers and leaves entwined on a trellis give variety and charm. The outer border and the field is suggestive of the classical trend. Colourings—central medallion field in a light brownish-pink, the general field in string colour with geometric motifs in yellows, and rims in shades of blue. Key-pattern border in tans, reds and yellows on light pinkish-brown.

coll.   Phillips of Hitchin Ltd.
lit.   *Country Life* (March 1962). An article dealing with Sawston Hall.

PLATE 52   **GEORGE III CARPET**   10ft. 5in. by 8ft. 7in.

3rd Quarter 18th Century—c. 1770

BY COURTESY OF MESSRS. FRANK PARTRIDGE AND SONS, LTD., LONDON

An 18th century carpet worked in *gros-point* in coloured wools with an all-over design of flowers and leaves in various colours on a brown ground. There is a wide trellis-pattern border with single flower heads, between two narrow borders, again suggestive of the Greek and Classical decoration beginning to make itself felt at this time. The floral centre emphasised effectively by the simple border.

PLATE 53   **GEORGE III CARPET**   6ft. 7in. by 6ft. 2in.

4th Quarter 18th Century—c. 1775

BY COURTESY OF MESSRS. PHILLIPS OF HITCHIN LTD.

Worked in tent-stitch and cross-stitch on a brown ground with yellow quatre foil design. There are floral motifs in polychrome colourings worked in silks and wools in the central medallion and corners. Embroidery is in red, blue and white in good shades of colour. The field and borders suggest a certain Greek influence. Certainly not later than 1775.

auct.   Christie's, London.
coll.   Arditti & Mayorcas, London.

PLATE 54   REGENCY PERIOD CARPET   12ft. 4in. by 10ft. 4in.

1st Quarter 19th Century—c. 1810

BY COURTESY OF MAYORCAS LTD., LONDON

An example of the Regency period, which can be placed at about the turn of the century and perhaps not later than 1810. Embroidered in coloured wools on a nutmeg brown ground. Interesting is the large medallion enclosing a smaller medallion. One notices scattered flowers in a chinoiserie style. It has three wide borders in yellows, reds, greens etc., on a rich rust ground. In this example one can clearly see an attempt at mixing a fading classical decor, with waning chinoiserie tendencies. Chinoiserie, well passed the zenith of its popularity, was kept alive fitfully by the interest of George, Prince of Wales.

PLATE 55   REGENCY RUG   5ft. 3in. by 3ft. 10in.

1st Quarter 19th Century—c. 1820

BY COURTESY OF THE EARL OF FEVERSHAM

A charming example of the Regency period, still showing much of the elegance and refinement of the eighteenth century. Delicate and pretty this rug is harmonious both in colour and design. It is worked in fresh natural colours in wool, in cross-stitch on six canvas squares. The Greek 'Key' pattern border is in celadon green outlined in soft yellow and divides the rug down the centre. The field, in parchment, is criss-crossed with a lattice design also in celadon green and outlined in yellow. Each square has a central nosegay of roses. From each corner, including those made by the joins with the central 'border', emerges a spray of roses and buds. These are complemented by another eight sprays which edge gently onto the field from the border at evenly-spaced intervals.

coll.   Arditti & Mayorcas, London.

PLATE 56   LATE GEORGIAN CARPET   7ft. 5in. by 6ft. 8in.

1st Quarter 19th Century—c. 1820

BY COURTESY OF MISS GRETA GARBO, NEW YORK

The paucity of design at this period, has none the less produced this pleasing example. It is worked in cross-stitch on three canvas widths, the whole enclosed in a border designed for it, but embroidered on a separate canvas. The pattern is composed of three bands of interlaced and foliated strap scrolls, supporting symmetrical clusters of scrolling leafage. The colours are in very pleasing shades of reds, blues, greens, yellows etc., on a gold coloured ground. The border in apple green with a pattern of a rod frame entwined with spirals of yellow leafage. This is the period of the revival—the Gothic revival starting from Strawberry Hill, the Rennaissance revival, the Rococo revival, in fact the revival of almost any former period. Here we see it: the Rococo with an attempt at Gothic and the Classical.

coll.   Arditti & Mayorcas, London.
             Ohan Berberyan, New York.
exhib.   Antique Dealers Fair 1959, London.
auct.   Parke-Bernet Galleries Inc., New York. Nov. 19th 1959. Lot 20 Illus.

PLATE 57GEORGIAN CARPET

1st Quarter 19th Century—c. 1825

BY COURTESY OF MESSRS. E. PEREZ (LONDON) LTD.

Forty-nine square panels joined together with a border form this large carpet. Each octagonal panel has various bunches of flowers. The whole enclosed in a conventional leaf pattern border. In naturalistic colours, and worked in a mixture of cross-stitch and tent-stitch. Where the squares join, a formal effect is created by the interspersion of ornate bosses. This is a good example of the mixing of the Gothic revival (ornate bosses), Classicism by the octagonal shaped panels, and lastly an attempted revival of Rococo by the 'C' leaf pattern border.

PLATES 58 and 59 GEORGE IV CARPET 9ft. 4in. by 8ft. 6in.

originally 11ft. 4in. by 10ft. 6in.

1st Quarter 19th Century—c. 1825

BY COURTESY OF AMEDEO DI CASTRO, ROME, ITALY

Carried out in cross-stitch on linen canvas in pleasant shades of rose pinks, greenish browns, etc. It has a tile pattern of quincunzes, centreing small crosses in scarlet and yellow. This suggests that originally it could have perhaps been made for use in a convent or church. The mosaic effect is achieved by the use of architectural bosses. Originally this carpet had a treble border and we are fortunate in being able to illustrate this as it was (Plate 58) and also as it is now with a single border only (Plate 59). It can be seen that one owner has had the two outer borders removed to give a more balanced effect with the field. The design is once again based on a Gothic revival with its bosses and quincunzes. Its classical borders (as originally made) are obviously a poor imitation of those at their peak in the late part of the 18th century. This style seems to point to the later geometrical patterns to appear in Victorian needlework. When auctioned in New York it was attributed to Scottish provenance, but there is no supporting evidence for this. A note in the sale catalogue said '*A larger carpet, of closely similar design, was in the collection of the Marquess of Breadalbane, Dalmally, Argyllshire*'.

coll.   Vigo Art Galleries, London.
        Ohan Berberyan, New York.
        Mrs. George Yetter, Savannah, U.S.A.
auct.   Parke-Bernet Galleries Inc., New York.
        28th October 1961. Lot 42 (with single border).

PLATE 60 GEORGE IV RUG 7ft. 6in. by 6ft. in.

1st Quarter 19th Century—c. 1825

BY COURTESY OF THE HERITAGE FOUNDATION, AND LOCATED AT DEERFIELD, MASSACHUSETTS

In the Dwight Barnard House at Deerfield, Mass., U.S.A. is this unusual geometric example of c. 1825. It is worked in wool on a white ground in navy blue and red in cross-stitch on three lengths of canvas.

It has a recticulated ground with a stylized red floral motif enclosed within diamond shapes formed by blue wavy strap borders with deep cream dots. The red zig-zag strap pattern main border, on a white ground with red dots, has two guards in red and blue chevron design, also on a white ground.

Where the rug is worn, the canvas is clearly seen to be a one-thread one size mesh weave and appears to be very white. This could be of course because it has been bleached—in which case it must be one of the very early bleached canvases, before the double-thread two size mesh appeared. The design is reminiscent of the early 17th century Italian velvets. Since it is not of this period it must be of the early part of the 19th century, when such designs were revived.

coll.   David Stockwell, Wilmington, Del. U.S.A.

PLATE 61   19th CENTURY CARPET   8ft. by 4ft. 7in.
1st Quarter 19th Century—c. 1825
BY COURTESY OF THE TRUSTEES OF THE LADY LEVER ART GALLEY, PORT SUNLIGHT

From the Lady Lever collection (Museum No. X912). Another carpet of the revival period. Worked in coloured wools on canvas, it is designed with diamond panels, scrolls, honeysuckle, bell ornaments, etc. The pleasing colours of the centre in reds, blues, blacks, etc., on a drab ground are set off very well by the border with drab again predominating, the border having an adaption of the eternal 'C'.

PLATE 62   19th CENTURY CARPET   10ft. by 7ft.
2nd Quarter 19th Century—c. 1830
BY COURTESY OF THE VICTORIA AND ALBERT MUSEUM

A very good example from perhaps the end of the first quarter of the century or the beginning of the second. This carpet is worked in tent-stitch in coloured wools on a linen canvas. The colours are very pleasing and are of the type associated with this period. The design of foliage is composed entirely in the manner of the rococo revival at its peak. This type of composition—La Rocaille in France—was very common in French decor in the early part of the 18th century. Beds with their ornate furnishings, curtains, spreads, etc., were all embroidered with this design.

PLATE 63   19th CENTURY 'QUEEN ANNE' REVIVAL   4ft. 6in. by 1ft. 9in.
2nd Quarter 19th Century—c. 1830
BY COURTESY OF MESSRS. ARDITTI & MAYORCAS LTD., LONDON

An overall pattern of various flowers on a tête-de-nègre field covers this window (or cupboard) rug of the 'Queen Anne' revival period. It has red peonies, red chrysanthemums, off-white carnations, pink tulips, and olive green foliage with touches of blue fading to soft green[1]. The outside guard border is in red and gold. The whole is worked in tent-stitch on two panels of double size mesh unbleached canvas.

The rather poor dyes indicate that this rug is not of the 18th century. This is endorsed by the familiar points, such as the double size mesh canvas, uncharacteristic layout, and the inferior quality of the wool.

---

[1] See Plates No. 64, 73.

PLATE 64   'QUEEN ANNE' REVIVAL TABLE COVER   5ft. 6in. by 4ft. 10in.
2nd Quarter 19th Century—c. 1830
BY COURTESY OF MESSRS. MAYORCAS LTD., LONDON

An exceedingly good example of the 'Queen Anne' revival which took place at the beginning of the 19th century. A further revival of 'Queen Anne' decor took place in the 1880's and 90's. This charming needlework table cover is on a peacock blue ground[1] fading in places to soft green with parts in the centre in old gold. It is worked on unbleached double mesh size canvas (which gives an approximate indication of its date). It is embroidered on three strips of canvas, in coarsish cross-stitch in fresh colours. Bright red peonies, carnations in natural colourings, yellow sunflowers and green and blue fading in places to soft green foliage cover the entire field.
The border of yellow sexagonal lozenges with red cruciform centres and white spots is finished by a two-tone blue outside guard.
Although this might at first sight appear to be of the early eighteenth century, a closer examination soon establishes this to be untrue. The design is a little 'muddy' and rather too informal. The canvas as mentioned is a very firm indication of the 19th century. The dyes and wools together with the fact that the colours have faded unevenly and inconsistently leaves virtually no doubt.

PLATE 65   GEORGIAN CARPET   9ft. 6in. by 6ft. 6in.
2nd Quarter 19th Century—c. 1830
BY COURTESY OF MESSRS. SALTI AND MODIANO, LONDON

This is a most pleasing composition, designed in concentric form, suggestive of its original purpose being that of a table carpet or, possibly, a ceiling carpet. Worked in coloured wools in coarse cross-stitch on three widths of canvas, the colours consist mainly of reds, blues, yellows, parchment on a jet black ground. The central medallion, depicting a Shepherdess in pastoral setting, is a blatant revival of the designs of this type so popular about 100 years prior. The scene is enclosed by scrolled strapwork. The rest of the field is strewn with a variety of large blooms, carnations, roses, sun flowers and foliage. Each corner has a centrally-facing exotic bird, enclosed in a cartouche. The wide outer border is composed of trailing blooms, carnations, roses, sunflowers, and cornered with a complementary set of cartouches, this time enclosing a small floral spray. Inside this large border are two narrow galloons, one of scrolling strapwork, in red and blue, and the other a chevron design, in red and parchment.

PLATE 66   WILLIAM IV CARPET   8ft. 1in. by 6ft. 4in.
2nd Quarter 19th Century—c. 1835
BY COURTESY OF E. B. SOUHAMI, LONDON

A carpet of very pleasing character, with a slightly French design of baskets and bows and floral wreaths. In cross-stitch on canvas, on a tête-de-nègre ground. It has a series of bow knotted golden rings hung with garlands of colourful roses and other flowers. In the centre a hanging basket of red roses and blue blossoms very akin to the floral baskets used by Phillipe de Lasalle in his woven silks at Lyons. The central design is enclosed within a double frame border. The corners finished with baskets of roses tied prettily to the border. The whole completed by a narrow plain yellow

1 See Plate No. 63, 73.

51

galloon in cross stitch. This again is a revival of the early 18th century shepherd and shepherdess designs. Its colours include pleasant reds, greens, yellows etc., but it has a solid green that was not introduced until 1835.

coll.   J. M. Pontremoli, London.
        Ohan Berberyan, New York, U.S.A.
auct.   Parke-Bernet Galleries Inc., New York. 28th Jan 1960. Ill. No. 24.

PLATE 67   19th CENTURY CHINOISERIE CARPET   9ft. 1½in. by 8ft. 9in.
                    2nd Quarter 19th Century—c. 1835
            BY COURTESY OF THE METROPOLITAN MUSEUM OF ART, NEW YORK

This is an interesting carpet for it portrays the Chinoiserie taste indulged in by George, Prince of Wales, which continued to about 1837. It is in itself a very pleasing carpet worked in cross-stitch on canvas. The central plain field contains a circular bunch of flowers and nothing else. Enclosed by a floral border of small flowers and leaves in pastel shades, it has a plain parchment background. The whole akin in design to the later Chinese embroideries which were imported into this country. It was given to the Metropolitan Museum by Mrs. J. V. McMullan, 1959.

PLATE 68   19th CENTURY CARPET   24ft. by 13ft. 7in.
                    2nd Quarter 19th Century—c. 1835
            BY COURTESY OF MRS. C. J. DEVINE, LLEWELLYN PARK, N.J., U.S.A.

On a bone white field, worked in cross-stitch in polychrome wools, on canvas squares. This carpet attributed to this country certainly has the features of a French Altar or Church carpet. However it has been included, for its general history seems to show otherwise. The squares embroidered in soft colours, with bouquets of mixed roses, morning glories of yellowish-green leafage and variegated other flowers, form a mosaic pattern. The intersections of formalized floral ornament finish in a cruciform manner. The double border has a tête de negré ground with a white leaf pattern.

coll.   Invereil House, Dirleton, East Lothian, Scotland.
        Sir Charles William Campbell, Bart.
        Marquess of Breadalbane, Craig, Dalmally, Argyll, Scotland
        Ohan Berberyan, New York.
N.B.—There are several reproductions of this carpet in existence.

PLATE 69   ARMORIAL CARPET   9ft. 6in. by 7ft. 6in.
                    2nd Quarter 19th Century—c. 1840
            BY COURTESY OF COLONIAL WILLIAMSBURG, VIRGINIA, U.S.A.

This armorial polychrome woollen rug worked in cross-stitch and tent-stitch on canvas, on a brown field, has symmetrically arranged squares radiating quatrefoils outlined in tan. The centre, depicting the arms of Great Britain[1], encircled by the Garter, and inscribed 'Honi soit qui mal y pense'. The

---

[1]There is a very interesting feature, in its central armorial crest. Williment's Regal Heraldry, up to the time of George IV does not show the Royal Arms in this form. It seems to be an unsuccessful attempt at portraying the arms of one of the Stuart Kings. The inaccuracy lies in the fact that, in this crest, the Irish Harp is taking precedence over the Scottish Lion, which is shown within a single tressure flory counter flory. In all accepted versions of the Stuart Royal Arms, the Scottish Lion comes before the Irish Harp, and the Scottish Lion is shown within a double tressure flory counter flory. It could of course be a simple inaccurate rendering of the arms in innocence.

field is covered with floral clusters in shades of blue, red, yellow and green, with a thistle and foliage at each corner. The border on a blue ground, has a floral trailing pattern of lillies, tulips, poppies, lilacs, and narcissi, in natural colours with green leaves, emerging from cornucopia at each corner. The cornucopeias are worked in red, yellow and tan. Each border has in the centre a tan octagonal medallion in tent-stitch, two containing patera and the opposite two fleur-de-lys. The design of architectural motifs, combined with floral patterns is typical of the 1840's, being a good example of the late Gothic revival, which had begun to wane somewhat.

coll.   Mrs. Coriat, 'Twatley', Malmesbury, Wiltshire.

PLATE 70   19th CENTURY CARPET   5ft. 10in. by 7ft. 6in.
                          2nd Quarter 19th Century—c. 1840
           BY COURTESY OF MRS. PAUL MAGNUSON, WASHINGTON, D.C., U.S.A.

In cross-stitch on canvas. The central field contains a floral bunch in the middle and this is surrounded by cartouches, two with parrots, two with birds. There is a three-masted sailing ship, and some swans upon placid water. The two cartouches at each end portray country scenes. A border encloses the carpet and is worked in a scrolling leaf design. The border is particularly interesting, for it shows once again the rococo revival—the eternal 'C' and by its centre it foreshadows the shape of things to come.

PLATE 71   STAINED GLASS WINDOW CARPET   14ft. 2in. by 13ft. 10in.
                          2nd Quarter 19th Century—c. 1840
           BY COURTESY OF THE CITY AND COUNTY OF KINGSTON-UPON-HULL MUSEUMS

A very unusual mid 19th century carpet worked in cross-stitch on canvas in reds, greens, pinks, blues, ambers and purple. The centre a mass of pink roses on lobed medallions to give an effect of stained glass windows. The border of grapes and foliage. One notes the Gothic tracery similar to the windows of churches. This is the only example that I have been able to trace of the carpets which were worked in the middle of the second quarter of the 19th century (or thereabouts) in a manner suggestive of stained glass windows. There were many made on the continent, in France in particular. Needless to say I have not included any of these. They were delightful to look at in spite of the fact that the revival of the Gothic emanating from Strawberry Hill was coming to a close. This carpet can be seen in The Victorian period room at Wilberforce House, High Street, Hull.

coll.   Arthur Jeffress, 1962.
auct.   Sotheby's London April 1962.

PLATE 72   EARLY VICTORIAN CARPET   17ft. by 11ft.
                          2nd Quarter 19th Century—c. 1840
           COURTESY OF MRS. F. H. FRELINGHUYSEN, MORRISTOWN, NEW JERSEY, U.S.A.

An exceptionally fine carpet which could be of French origin, but because of its treatment has been included as a possible English example.
It has a pattern of simple scrolled lozenges and decorative floral bouquets in naturalistic colourings, interspersed with rosettes of alternate design. Worked in cross-stitch in coloured wools on canvas squares. It is shown in its setting at the home of the owner, Mrs. Frelinghuysen in New Jersey, U.S.A.

coll.   Ohan Berberyan, New York.

A most curious mid 19th century carpet is on exhibition at The Welsh Folk Museum in Cardiff. It is worked in coarse cross-stitch on five lengths of a sacking like canvas, probably made of hemp. The ground is in off-white wool, the design in red, pale blue and a little brown. The blue has faded to the palest of green[1]. This is a peculiarity of the blue dyes of this period and applies also to twentieth century restorations that have been carried out in blue wools. The pattern is of interlacing wavy lines with vase motifs in the corners, having in the centre an eight petalled formal flower head.

The design of this carpet is a good example of some of the rather confused inaccurate 'revivals' which were the basis of much of the early 19th century decorative art. The stylized central motif, which is obviously a Classical emblem, has been deluged by the profusion of straight, wavy and concentric lines. The complete incongruity is emphasised by the four corner vase motifs, a tentative reminder of the bold Italianate designs of the 17th century. Yet, as has been said before, such aesthetically wrong and impure designs are not without a charm of their own.

Formerly in the possession of the Earls of Powis, it is said that this rug was worked by members of the family and was formerly in use at Walcot in Shropshire.

coll.   Earl of Powis.

This large carpet is an exceedingly good example of English Needlework at the beginning of the 1840's. It is the work of many hands and is carried out in cross-stitch on canvas squares and finished with a border of a rod frame with entwined leaf. It contains 77 panels worked alternately on a puce and white field, with narrow red and gold borders. Each square has a different motif, comprising birds, flowers, crests, etc. The centre panel bears two shields of arms, one the arms of Gloucester and Bristol and the other the arms borne by James Henry Monk, Bishop of Gloucester and Bristol (1830-1856) which should be 'Gu; a chevron between three Lion's heads, erased, arg'. Since he was married (to Jane, daughter of the Rev. Hugh Hughes, of Nuneaton, Warwicks., in 1823) he also bore another shield, placed sinister to the other, with his own arms and those of his wife. Burke's *General Armory* 3rd edition, gives the arms of the Rev. Hugh Hughes as follows: 'Erm. a Lion ramp. gu. with a bordure sa. fretty or' Incidentally, Monk's arms were those borne by Viscount Monck. This carpet was presented to Bishop Monk in 1843 and the following announcement appears in *Felix Farley's Bristol Journal*, Saturday, December 23rd, 1843:

'On Saturday Dec. 9, a beautiful carpet, of Berlin worsted work, was presented by several ladies of the county and City of Gloucester to the Bishop of the diocese and his lady, at Tolzey, Gloucester, as an offering of their grateful sense of the Bishop's and Mrs. Monk's uniform hospitality and obliging attentions to all the families of the extensive circle of their acquaint-

---

[1] See Plates No. 63, 64.

ance. This splendid and unique present consisted of 77 large squares of puce and white ground alternately, on which was worked some device of flowers, fruit or birds, except the centre-piece, which contained the armorial bearings, each contributed by a different lady, according to her own taste; and although several squares were worked at home, without reference to one another, they afterwards formed, when put together, a *tout assemble*, about 24 feet in length, and 16 in breadth, of the most harmonious colours and designs. The effect of the whole was no less pleasing to the eye, as a picture, than gratifying to the feelings, as a testimonial, having been produced with no little time and trouble, by the fair hands of numerous ladies of the highest respectability, out of compliment to the Diocesan and his lady'.

The *Bristol Mirror* for the same date, gives an identical account, and adds that the presentation took place between twelve and one o'clock.

Reports of this event in *The Gloucester Journal* and *The Gloucestershire Chronicle* varying very little from the above were also given. Unfortunately none reported the names of the ladies involved. Bishop Monk died at Stapleton Palace in 1856.

repr.   F. Lewis—*Oriental Carpets and Textiles—The Perez Collection*, 1953. Frontispiece.
auct.   Sotheby's, London, 25th May 1951.
coll.   James Henry Monk, Bishop of Gloucester and Bristol (1830-1856).
         Lt. Colonel G. A. Sanford, 1951.
         E. Perez (London) Ltd.

PLATE 75   EARLY VICTORIAN CARPET   11ft. 1in. by 9ft. 5in.
                          2nd Quarter 19th Century—c. 1843
                    BY COURTESY OF MR. JOHN V. SANGSTER, LONDON

A number of 'kettle-holders', squares and border make up this most interesting composition, interesting because of its charm and its date. Each panel is worked separately in *petit-point* in polychrome wools on canvas, then contained within the border worked separately. It was the habit of the producers of printed fabrics, the Staffordshire potters, the fan-makers, and so on, to portray naval and military occasions, events and scenes of the times in their wares. This carpet does this extremely well and can be looked upon as a 'mirror of the time.'

coll.   E. Perez (London) Ltd. (c. 1950).
repr.   F. Lewis—*Oriental Rugs and Textiles—The Perez Collection* p. 9 and plate 48.

PLATE 76   VICTORIAN CARPET   5ft. 6in. by 3ft. 6in.
                          2nd Quarter 19th Century—c. 1845
                BY COURTESY OF MESSRS. ROFFÉ & RAPHAEL, THE VIGO ART GALLERIES

Needlework rug, of natural colourings, worked in polychrome wools on canvas. The backgrounds of the squares are in pale blue, black or white. This is obviously an example of the early part of the Victorian period, when lightness of design was still the aim. Each little square is a charming picture in its own right, and together they combine in a superb harmony of colour and subject. Despite a disarming naivety, there is a simplified naturalness which is most attractive. The rug is worked in very fine cross-stitch 'kettle-holders'.

PLATE 77   VICTORIAN RUG   5ft. 2in. by 5ft. 6in.
2nd Quarter 19th Century—signed C.P.B.F. and dated 1848

BY COURTESY OF QUALITY WOOD, OUSDEN, NEWMARKET

An interesting example of the early Victorian 'geometric' design rugs. This, of course, is yet another manifestation of the unquenchable Victorian desire for copying, rekindling, or adapting. In this case, the obvious source is the traditional designs of the Caucasian carpets and rugs with their simple stylized central motif, surrounded by any number of intricate, geometric borders. Naturally the pattern has here been somewhat modified, or 'Victorianised', some of the borders being distinctly recognisable as of English origin. It is always intriguing to try to fathom out just how much of the inaccuracies of Victorian copying was deliberate adaptation to suit current taste, and how much slack craftmanship.

The central stylized flower motif is worked in reds, blues and whites, on a pistachio green ground. The eleven surrounding borders are on red, black or white, with the various designs in greens, blues, yellows and browns. The rug is worked in coloured wools on cotton canvas, in cross-stitch. An added interest is the date 1848 and C.P.B.F. in the bottom left hand corner, presumably the worker's initials.

PLATE 78   VICTORIAN CARPET   10ft. by 7ft.
2nd Quarter 19th Century—c. 1850

BY COURTESY OF MESSRS. ROFFÉ & RAPHAEL, THE VIGO ART GALLERIES, LONDON

A fine Victorian needlework carpet, with well-drawn designs worked on separate squares of canvas. Polychrome wools are worked in fine cross-stitch, and the border is composed of gold tassels with a small floral cartouche in each corner. The overall impression is a pleasingly informal pattern of animals, birds and flowers, charmingly lacking in symmetry and completely without the pretentious pomp of later Victoriana. The Victorians seemed passionately fond of dogs and they were used frequently in embroidery.

PLATE 79   VICTORIAN CARPET   9ft. by 7ft.
2nd Quarter 19th Century—c. 1850

BY COURTESY OF MESSRS. ROFFÉ & RAPHAEL, THE VIGO ART GALLERIES, LONDON

A floral Victorian needlework carpet, worked in squares on canvas, and executed in polychrome wools in cross-stitch. The multi-coloured floral motifs are each on a white ground, alternating with a brown and black stylised pattern. It will be observed each bouquet is slightly different in design and floral arrangement.

PLATE 80 & 81   VICTORIAN CARPET   14ft. 11in. by 11ft. 11in.
3rd Quarter 19th Century—c. 1851

BY COURTESY OF MESSRS. J. HAIM LTD., LONDON

This most attractive carpet is worked in cross-stitch on canvas, divided into seven rows of squares. Each square is enclosed by blue ribbon with a red diamond in each corner. The whole carpet including the field is worked in a profusion of gay colourings. The squares contain floral and bird motifs, including cornucopia and bouquets of summer flowers, such as morning glory, lillies, violets, convolvulus and lilac, together with an occasional parrot. The arcaded border is in yellow and sepia.

The carpet is given added interest and authenticity by an accompanying plan (Plate 81), which gives definite proof of the co-operative fashion in which this, as well as certainly many other carpets of this period, were worked. The plan shows the proposed subject of each individual square, and also the name of the worker. The reverse of the plan is inscribed:-

'Description of a carpet worked by Miss Willis and her Friends and given by her to her Goddaughter Emily Ann Powell on her marriage October 28th 1851'.

coll.   S. K. M. Powell, 1962.

auct.   Sotheby & Co., London, 11 May, 1962 (203).

PLATE 82   A VICTORIAN CARPET   13ft. 4in. by 9ft. 4in.

3rd Quarter 19th Century—c. 1855

BY COURTESY OF MR. V. H. JINISHIAN, NEW YORK

Another carpet continuing the theme in Plate Nos. 85 and 86, comprising 54 squares and a repeating leaf-design border terminating, in the corners, with a five-leaf motif boss. Entirely worked on canvas squares in tent-stitch in polychrome wools on a bone white ground, it makes a very effective and charming floor covering. The design mainly of a floral character, is made up of varying kinds of blooms arranged in different kinds of bunches and interspersed here and there with birds of different species sitting on branches or floral twigs. The layout of the carpet points to a convent or perhaps altar use originally by virtue of its shape and the cruciform intersections.

coll.   E. Perez (London) Ltd.

PLATE 83   AN EARLY VICTORIAN TILE CARPET   12ft. by 12ft.

3rd Quarter 19th Century—c. 1855.

BY COURTESY OF LORD OGILVY

A fine example of the high development of the designs originating with the competition held by the R.S.A. in conjunction with the Exhibition at the Crystal Palace in 1851. This carpet is woven entirely in cross-stitch on canvas squares in polychrome wools. It has 32 squares containing various arrangements of floral bouquets in fresh colourings with the corner sections on a red ground. The intersections forming a rosette akin to stained glass. The centre of the carpet is taken up by a huge tile-like form (in size equal to four squares) canvas square on which is embroidered a vase standing on a field and containing a large assortment of flowers. The border of trailing leaf form in natural colours on a red ground is completed at the corners in a manner again suggestive of stained glass. Photograph shows quarter detail. At Cortochy Castle.

coll.   Arditti & Mayorcas, London.

PLATE 84 VICTORIAN CARPET 15ft. by 13ft. 3in.
3rd Quarter 19th Century—c. 1855
BY COURTESY OF J. HAIM & CO., LONDON

The sixth decade of the 19th century saw quite a number of these 'Tile' carpets and this one follows the general trend. It is worked on canvas squares in polychrome wools in fine cross-stitch. The squares at the intersections terminating in rosettes, are enclosed within a double narrow frame border with a formal design. The interesting variety of designs comprise all kinds of floral bouquets, all manner of dogs, figures and one with a standing woman with a harp. A most pleasing ensemble, carried out in natural colours.

coll. Marquis of Breadalbane.
auct. Messrs. Christie Manson & Woods, London.
illus. *Connoisseur,* June 1958.

PLATE 85 VICTORIAN CARPET 14ft. by 8ft. 6in.
3rd Quarter 19th Century—c. 1855
BY COURTESY OF MESSRS. ROFFÉ & RAPHAEL, THE VIGO ART GALLERIES, LONDON

A fine needlework carpet, worked in polychrome wools in cross-stitch on canvas, woven as squares and joined on completion. The multi-coloured floral bouquets are on white octagons in light blue backgrounds. The ribbon border is in deep rose on white. The charm of this carpet rests in its freshness of colour and simplicity of design, the whole being skilfully and unobtrusively rounded off by so plain and undistracting a border.

PLATE 86 VICTORIAN CARPET 7ft. 9in. by 5ft. 8in.
3rd Quarter 19th Century—c. 1855
BY COURTESY OF MRS. LYTLE HULL, RHINEBECK-ON-HUDSON, NEW YORK

Fifteen squares embroidered on canvas, worked in polychrome wools in cross-stitch. This delightful composition of tiles enclosed within a fret border with rosettes at each intersection is typical of the carpets produced in the sixth decade of the 19th century. Each of the fifteen panels shows a different motif of dogs, flowers, birds, etc. The *genre* of this design has been ascribed to one of the early competitions for carpet designs held by the Royal Society of Arts at about the time of the Great Exhibition, held in the Crystal Palace in Hyde Park in 1851.

coll. Ohan Berberyan, New York.

PLATE 87 VICTORIAN CARPET 9ft. 10in. by 7ft. 9in.
3rd Quarter—19th Century—c. 1860
BY COURTESY OF MRS. WILLIAM RUSSELL GRACE, AIKEN, S. CAROLINA, U.S.A.

A large fireplace carpet worked in cross-stitch on canvas in polychrome wools on canvas strips. The central panel enclosed by a twisted ribbon frame contains a large garland of various flowers, with a big daffodil in the centre. In one corner of the wreath is a passion flower. The border a trailing floral pattern with a white lily as the repeating theme. The lily so beloved of the Victorians together with the treatment of the central garland shows the beginning of true Victoriana.

coll. Ohan Berberyan, New York.

PLATE 88   VICTORIAN RUG   5ft. 9in. by 2ft. 8in.
                        3rd Quarter 19th Century—c. 1860
                   BY COURTESY OF MESSRS. MAYORCAS LTD., LONDON

A simple rug on a black ground, with a floral rope border. Worked in cross-stitch with polychrome
wools of exceedingly fresh colour, on canvas. The centre enclosed by a thin yellow line, is composed of a bunch of roses, flanked by two floral wreaths. Again a development from earlier designs
and portrayed in a true Victorian fashion. With the 1850's there began a trend for black backgrounds—this is an early example.

PLATE 89   VICTORIAN CARPET   12ft. by 8ft. 2in.
                        3rd Quarter 19th Century—c. 1860
                   BY COURTESY OF THE VICTORIA AND ALBERT MUSEUM

A large carpet in cross-stitch, Museum No. T. 172-1930. It is worked in polychrome wools, on
canvas; there are 6 stitches to the inch, which corresponds to 40 knots to the inch in a pile carpet.
The pattern and field in cross-stitch. The closely packed large red roses and green leaves—perhaps
burdock—leave very little of the black ground showing. The 6 circular medallions on a white
ground contain a round bunch of naturalistic flowers. A pleasant, florid design typical of the middle
of the 19th century, with its large floral nosegays, its big leaves etc., its exotic flowers, its black
ground all common in the late 50's and early 60's.

PLATE 90   VICTORIAN CARPET   9ft. 4in. by 7ft. 6in.
                        3rd Quarter 19th Century—c. 1860
                   BY COURTESY OF MISS DORIS DUKE, CALIFORNIA, U.S.A.

A very fine example of floral Victoriana; this needlework carpet is worked in cross-stitch in
coloured wools of a fresh colour, on canvas squares. The border has a trailing floral pattern interspersed with lillies between a narrow frame galloon. It has fourteen framed squares, and on a black
ground nosegays of various blooms in natural colours. The central motif—a canvas square equal
in size to six of those already used in this carpet—has an oval floral mass of peonies, roses, lillies
and other flowers, with quarter circular floral garlands in the corners. True Victoriana at its peak,
showing the floral motifs as if in relief.
N.B. Mrs. Alan Corey, former owner of this very fine Victorian example replaced it with a reproduction. The reproduction omits the floral border.
coll.   Mrs. Alan L. Corey, Jr.
           Ohan Berberyan, New York.

PLATE 91   VICTORIAN RUG   7ft. 5in. by 5ft. 1in.
                        3rd Quarter 19th Century—c. 1860
                 BY COURTESY OF MRS. STEPHEN C. CLARK JR., MIDDLEBURG, VIRGINIA, U.S.A.

Very similar to the central motif of Plate No. 92 this Victorian example is worked in cross-stitch
on canvas and finishes with a narrow rope pattern border. It has a large floral mass in the centre
with roses, interesting catkins, leaves and other flowers. In the corners L shaped garlands of similar

blooms. The freshness of the colours is accentuated on a black ground. The introduction of the large cabbage rose in Victorian designs at about the middle of the sixth decade is very prominent in their floor coverings, wallpapers, small firescreens and so on. It is more than likely a copy of the large cabbage rose used extensively in Louis XVI linens and cottons. A good example of florid Victoriana.

coll.   Ohan Berberyan, New York.
auct.   Parke-Bernet Galleries Inc., New York, 28 January, 1960. No. 28.

PLATE 92   VICTORIAN RUG   7ft. 6in. by 5ft. 9in.
3rd Quarter 19th Century—c. 1865

BY COURTESY OF MRS. STEPHEN C. CLARK JR., MIDDLEBURG, VIRGINIA, U.S.A.

A typical Victorian needlework rug of this time. Worked in cross-stitch in coloured wools on a tête de negré ground. The floral mass taking up the whole of rug is composed of roses, catkins, peonies, etc., with foliage in natural fresh colourings. Akin to Plate No. 91 minus the border, this begins to show the decline of Victoriana, with its introduction of exotic flowers, etc., in the late 60's early 70's.

coll.   Ohan Berberyan, New York, U.S.A.
auct.   Parke-Bernet Galleries Inc., New York, 19th November 1959. No. 15.

PLATE 93   VICTORIAN CARPET   13ft. 2in. by 9ft.
4th Quarter 19th Century—c. 1880

BY COURTESY OF THE TRYON PALACE, NEW BERN, NORTH CAROLINA, U.S.A.

This carpet is to be seen in the Alcove Bedroom of the magnificently restored Tryon Palace. We illustrate both a detail and the carpet shown in its setting. It is worked in cross-stitch on a pale gold ground, with plumes and flowers in light blue, rose and gold. A wide border, on a similar gold ground, is contained by two narrow 'guard' borders, of simple plumes and scrolls. The composition of the pattern is derived from symbols taken from famous historical rooms, hence the Peacock feathers from Marie-Antoinette's Peacock Throne, and the plumes from Cleopatra's boudoir, and Madame Dubarry's Fontainebleu. At first glance the carpet has a French appearance, but on further examination it could well be English.

coll.   Ohan Berberyan, New York.

PLATE 94   LATE VICTORIAN RUG   approx. 7ft. 6in. by 5ft.
4th Quarter 19th Century—c. 1890

BY COURTESY OF J. HAIM & CO., LONDON

This example is worked in cross-stitch on a parchment ground in naturalistic colours. The centre is taken up by a large parrot in fresh plumage sitting an a branch. The border, also on a parchment ground, has a pattern of trailing flowers with leaves interspersed with shells.

auct.   Messrs. Sotheby & Co., London.

Index of Owners

Messrs. Quality Wood - - - - - - - - 77
Messrs. Roffé & Raphael, London - - - - - 22, 76, 78, 79, 85
City Art Museum of St. Louis - - - - - - - 13
Messrs. Salti & Modiano - - - - - - - 65
Mr. John V. Sangster - - - - - - - 75
The Marquess of Salisbury - - - - - - - 4, 11, 34
Messrs. E. B. Souhami - - - - - - - 66
Tryon Palace, New Bern, N.C. - - - - - 32, 33, 93
Judge Irwin Untermyer - - - - - - 24, 39
Victoria and Albert Museum - - - 2, 5, 6, 7, 9, 10, 14, 18, 62, 89
Welsh Folk Museum, Cardiff (National Museum of Wales) - - - 73
Colonial Williamsburg, Virginia - - - - - 26, 27, 37, 45, 69

CORRECTIONS

PLATE 13.   d. 1615 *should read* c. 1615
PLATE 48.   c. 1765 *should read* d. 1765
PLATE 91.   d. 1860 *should read* c. 1860

OMISSIONS

It is regretted that the needlework carpets owned by The Earl of Mar and Kellie (2), and The Earl of Shaftesbury could not be illustrated, the details and photographs arriving too late for inclusion.

ILLUSTRATIONS

PLATE 1

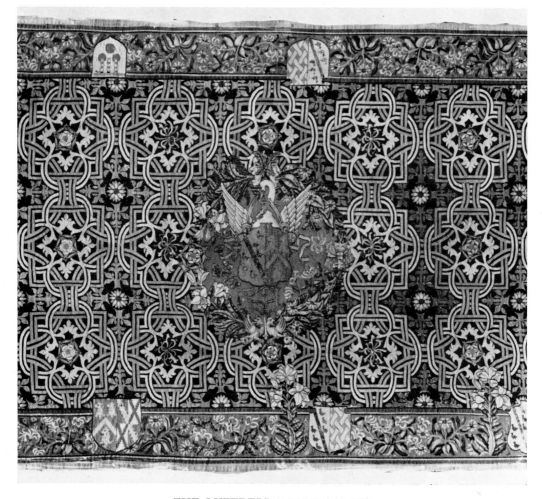

18'1" × 6'4"

THE LUTTRELL TABLE CARPET
By courtesy of Glasgow Museums & Art Galleries

C. 1520

PLATE 2

18′4″ × 4′6″   THE GIFFORD CARPET   c. 1550
By courtesy of the Victoria & Albert Museum

PLATE 3

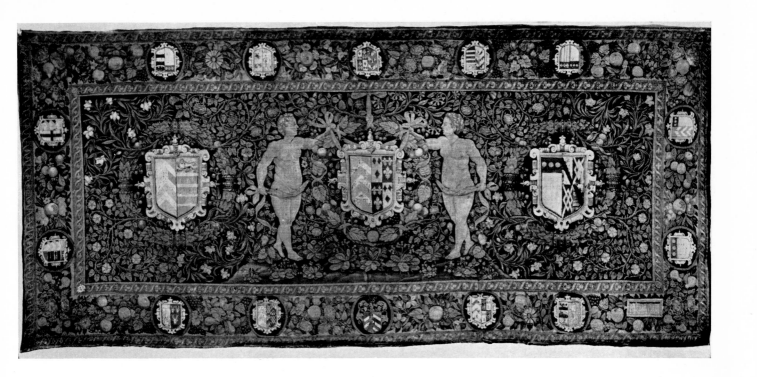

16'3" × 7'5"

THE LEWKENOR TABLE CARPET
By courtesy of The Metropolitan Museum of Art, New York

c. 1564

PLATE 4

9' × 9'

ELIZABETHAN TABLE CARPET

c. 1580

By courtesy of The Marquess of Salisbury

PLATE 5

9'5" × 4'10"   ELIZABETHAN CARPET   c. 1600
By courtesy of the Victoria & Albert Museum

PLATE 6

c. 1600

ELIZABETHAN TABLE CARPET
By courtesy of the Victoria & Albert Museum

9'9" × 5'6"

PLATE 7

13' × 5'9"

ELIZABETHAN TABLE CARPET
By courtesy of the Victoria & Albert Museum

c. 1600

PLATE 8

LATE 16TH CENTURY TABLE CARPET

By courtesy of Mr. C. F. J. Beausire

PLATE 9

4′10″ × 2′8″
TABLE CARPET FRAGMENT
c. 1600
By courtesy of the Victoria & Albert Museum

PLATE 10

ELIZABETHAN CARPET
By courtesy of the Victoria & Albert Museum

PLATE 11

6' × 4'8" JAMES I TABLE CARPET c. 1610
By courtesy of The Marquess of Salisbury

PLATE 12

11'9" × 8'5"

THE HULSE CARPET
By courtesy of Sir Westrow Hulse, Bart.

dated 1614

PLATE 13

11′1″ × 7′1½″   JAMES I TABLE CARPET   d. 1615
By courtesy of the City Art Museum, St. Louis

PLATE 14

13½″ × 5¼″   TABLE CARPET FRAGMENT   c. 1620
By courtesy of the Victoria & Albert Museum

PLATE 15

9′4″ × 6′2″ CHARLES I TABLE CARPET c. 1630
By courtesy of the City of Birmingham Museum & Art Gallery

PLATE 16

c. 1640

MID-17TH CENTURY TABLE CARPET
By courtesy of Mr. & Mrs. London, Paris

8'4" × 5'4"

PLATE 17

10'7" × 7'6"

CHARLES II TABLE CARPET
By courtesy of Mrs. J. M. Pontremoli

Dated 1661

PLATE 18

11′5″ × 7′8″ TURKEY WORK CARPET dated 1672
By courtesy of the Victoria & Albert Museum

PLATE 19

8′5″ × 5′4½″
QUEEN ANNE CARPET
c. 1705
By courtesy of Messrs: Phillips of Hitchin Ltd.

PLATE 20

7′6″ × 5′5″ *approx.*   QUEEN ANNE CARPET   C. 1710
Present ownership unknown

PLATE 21

7′11″ × 7′9″   QUEEN ANNE CARPET   C. 1710
Present ownership unknown

6′ × 4′6″   GEORGE I CARPET   c. 1720
By courtesy of Mrs. David Gubbay

PLATE 22

9′ × 7′ *approx.*   GEORGIAN CARPET   c. 1725
By courtesy of Messrs: Roffé & Raphael, The Vigo Art Galleries, London

PLATE 23

10'7" × 8'6" GEORGE II CARPET (with detail) Dated 1730
By courtesy of Mrs. David Gubbay

PLATE 24

10′9″ × 8′6″

GEORGE II VASE CARPET
By courtesy of Judge Irwin Untermyer, New York

c. 1730

PLATE 25

26′ × 16′   THE RABY CARPET   c. 1730
By courtesy of Lord Barnard

PLATE 26

EARLY GEORGIAN CARPET
By courtesy of Colonial Williamsburg, Virginia, U.S.A.

c. 1735

PLATE 27

The carpet on Plate 26 in its actual setting

PLATE 28

8′ × 8′ GEORGE II CARPET c. 1735
By courtesy of Mrs. David Gubbay

PLATE 29

9′ × 6′6″ GEORGIAN RUG c. 1735
By courtesy of the Heritage Foundation, Deerfield, Massachusetts, U.S.A.

PLATE 30

10′ × 8′ *approx.* GEORGE II CARPET c. 1740
By courtesy of Sir Hubert Medlycott, Bart.

PLATE 31

7'3" × 4'6"   EARLY GEORGIAN CARPET   c. 1740
By courtesy of The Trustees of The Lady Lever Art Gallery, Port Sunlight, Cheshire

PLATE 32

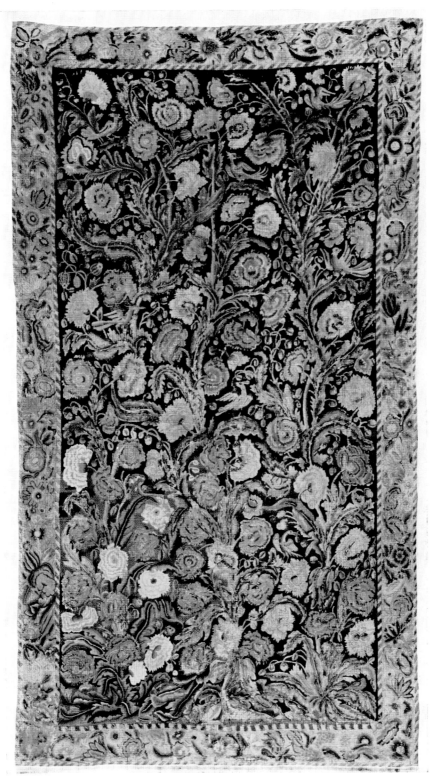

9'6" × 5'4"   GEORGE II CARPET   c. 1740
By courtesy of The Tryon Palace, New Bern, N.C., U.S.A.

PLATE 33

The carpet on Plate 32 in its actual setting

PLATE 34

9′ × 6′   HATFIELD HOUSE CARPET   c. 1740

By courtesy of The Marquess of Salisbury

PLATE 35

12'11" × 9'4"

GEORGE II TABLE CARPET
By courtesy of The Lord Fairhaven

c. 1740

PLATE 36

10′ × 7′   GEORGE II CARPET   c. 1740
By courtesy of The Trustees of The Lady Lever Art Gallery, Port Sunlight, Cheshire

PLATE 37

8′3″ × 7′6″

GEORGE II CARPET
By courtesy of Colonial Williamsburg, Virginia, U.S.A.

c. 1740

PLATE 38

11′ × 5′6″   GEORGE II CARPET   signed EN & dated 1743
By courtesy of The Metropolitan Museum of Art, New York

PLATE 39

7′8½″ × 7′4″   GEORGE II CARPET   signed HT & dated 6 Oct. 1743
By courtesy of Judge Irwin Untermyer, New York, U.S.A.

PLATE 40

15' × 9'6"   THE "HOLTE" CARPET—GEORGE II   c. 1744
By courtesy of The City of Birmingham Museum and Art Gallery

PLATE 41

14'6" × 12'8"

GEORGE II CARPET

c.1750

By courtesy of Messrs.: Frank Partridge & Sons Ltd., London

PLATE 42

6'7" × 4'10"

GEORGIAN CARPET
By courtesy of Mr. Benson Ford, Michigan, U.S.A.

c. 1755

PLATE 43

10′5″ × 8′9″ GEORGE II CARPET c. 1755
By courtesy of V. H. Jinishian, New York

PLATE 44

4′6″ × 2′1″ (each)

PAIR GEORGE III RUGS
In the possession of Messrs: Arditti & Mayorcas, London

c. 1760

PLATE 45

7′ × 5′6″   GEORGIAN CARPET   c. 1760
By courtesy of Colonial Williamsburg, Virginia, U.S.A.

PLATE 46

19′ × 12′ *approx.*   GEORGIAN CARPET   c. 1760
By courtesy of The Trustees of Harvard University

PLATE 47

Showing the carpet on plate 46 at The Royal School of Needlework, London after completion of repairs in 1954

PLATE 48

9′9″ × 8′10″

GEORGE III CARPET
By courtesy of The Metropolitan Museum of Art, New York

c. 1765

PLATE 49

10′ × 8′6″   GEORGE III CARPET   c. 1765
By courtesy of V. H. Jinishian, New York

PLATE 50

8′ × 6′4″   "CHINOISERIE" CARPET   c. 1765
                         By courtesy of Mrs. David Gubbay

PLATE 51

7′ × 5′9½″   GEORGE III CARPET   c. 1770
By courtesy of Captain R. F. Eyre Huddleston, R.N., and Mrs. Eyre Huddleston

PLATE 52

10′5″ × 8′7″   GEORGE III CARPET   c. 1770
By courtesy of Messrs.: Frank Partridge & Sons Ltd., London

PLATE 53

6'7" × 6'2"

GEORGE III CARPET
By courtesy of Messrs: Phillips of Hitchin Ltd.

c. 1775

PLATE 54

12'4" × 10'4"   REGENCY PERIOD CARPET   c. 1810
By courtesy of Messrs: Mayorcas Ltd, London

PLATE 55

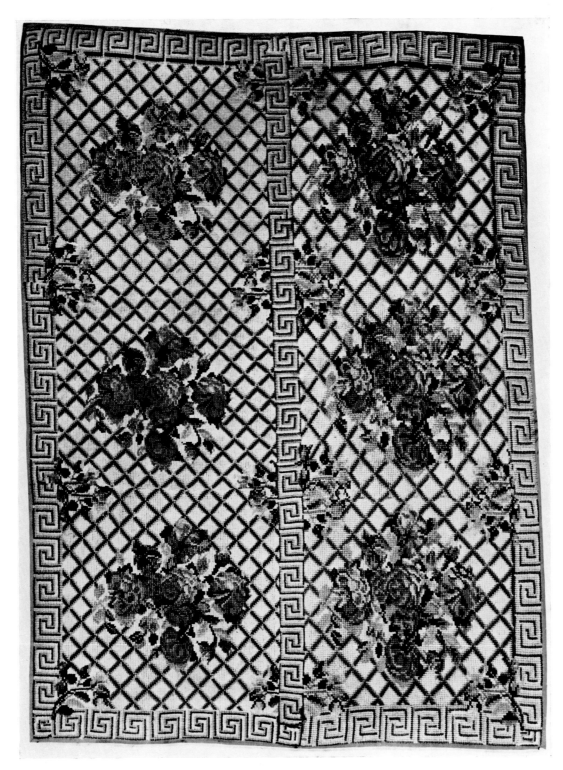

5′3″ × 3′10″   REGENCY RUG   c. 1820
By courtesy of The Earl of Feversham

PLATE 56

LATE GEORGIAN CARPET
By courtesy of Miss Greta Garbo, New York

PLATE 57

5'10" × 15'6"

GEORGIAN CARPET

c. 1825

By courtesy of Messrs: E. Perez (London) Ltd.

PLATE 58

11'4" × 10'6"   GEORGE IV CARPET (original state)   c. 1825
By courtesy of Amedeo Di Castro, Rome, Italy

PLATE 59

9′4″ × 8′6″

GEORGE IV CARPET (present state)
By courtesy of Amedeo Di Castro, Rome, Italy

c. 1825

PLATE 60

7′6″ × 6′6″   GEORGE IV RUG   c. 1825
By courtesy of the Heritage Foundation, Deerfield, Massachusetts, U.S.A.

PLATE 61

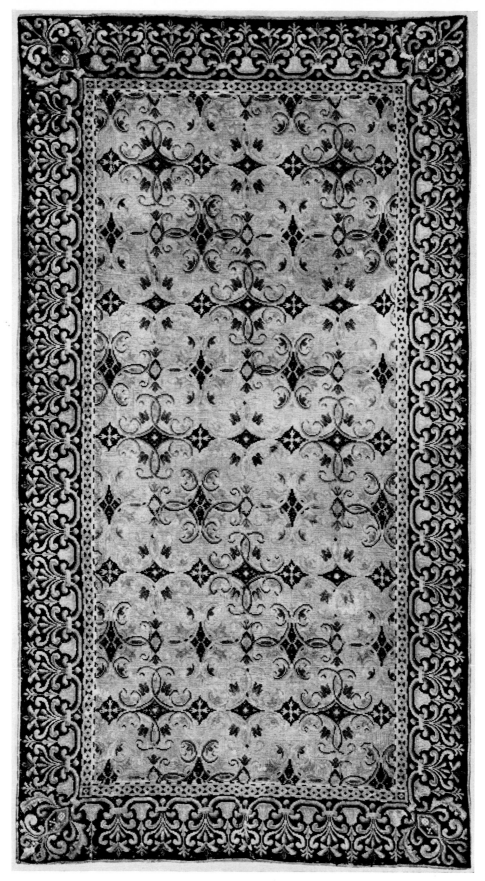

8′ × 4′7″　　　　19TH CENTURY CARPET　　　　c. 1825
By courtesy of The Trustees of The Lady Lever Art Gallery, Port Sunlight, Cheshire

PLATE 62

19TH CENTURY CARPET
By courtesy of The Victoria & Albert Museum

PLATE 63

4'6" × 1'9"   c. 1830
19TH CENTURY "QUEEN ANNE" REVIVAL
By courtesy of Messrs: Arditti & Mayorcas, London

PLATE 64

5′6″ × 4′10″ "QUEEN ANNE" REVIVAL TABLE COVER c. 1830
By courtesy of Messrs: Mayorcas Ltd, London

PLATE 65

9′6″ × 6′6″

GEORGIAN CARPET

c. 1830

By courtesy of Messrs: Salti & Modiano, London

PLATE 66

8'1" × 6'4" WILLIAM IV CARPET c. 1835
By courtesy of E. B. Souhami, London

PLATE 67

9′1½″ × 8′9″ 19TH CENTURY "CHINOISERIE" CARPET c. 1835
By courtesy of The Metropolitan Museum of Art, New York

PLATE 68

24′ × 13′7″　　　19TH CENTURY CARPET　　　c. 1835
By courtesy of Mrs. C. J. Devine, Llewellyn Park, N.J., U.S.A.

PLATE 69

9'6" × 7'6"   ARMORIAL CARPET   c. 1840
By courtesy of Colonial Williamsburg, Virginia, U.S.A.

PLATE 70

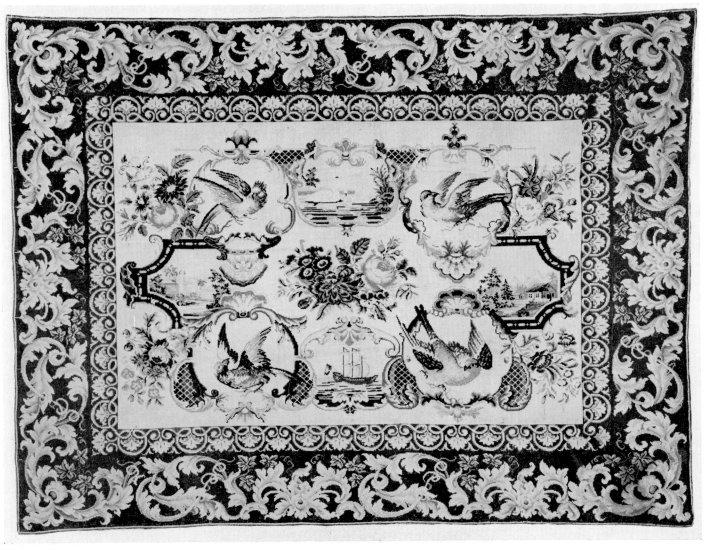

5'10" × 7'6"

19TH CENTURY CARPET
By courtesy of Mrs. Paul Magnuson, Washington D.C., U.S.A.

c. 1840

PLATE 71

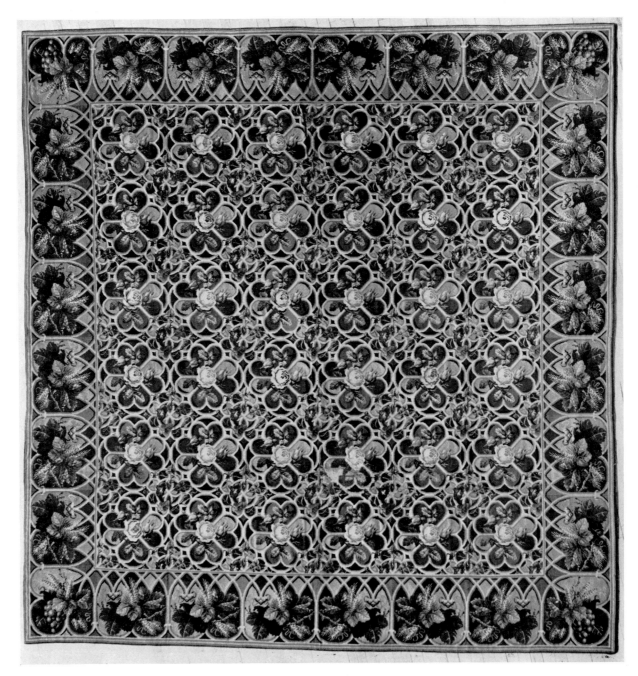

14'2" × 13'10"   STAINED GLASS WINDOW CARPET   c. 1840
By courtesy of The City and County of Kingston-upon-Hull Museums

PLATE 72

EARLY VICTORIAN CARPET
By courtesy of Mrs. F. H. Frelinghuysen, Morristown, N.J., U.S.A.

PLATE 73

12′ × 12′ *approx.*   19TH CENTURY "CLASSICAL" REVIVAL   c. 1840
By courtesy of Amgueddfa Werin Cymru—Welsh Folk Museum

" × 14'10"

THE BISHOP MONK VICTORIAN CARPET
By courtesy of V. H. Jinishian, New York

PLATE 75

11′1″ × 9′5″

EARLY VICTORIAN CARPET
By courtesy of Mr. John V. Sangster, London

c. 1843

PLATE 76

5'6" × 3'6"

VICTORIAN CARPET
By courtesy of Messrs: Roffé & Raphael, The Vigo Art Galleries, London

c. 1845

PLATE 77

5′2″ × 5′6″
VICTORIAN RUG
By courtesy of Quality Wood, Ousden, Newmarket
dated 1848

PLATE 78

10′ × 7′   VICTORIAN CARPET   c. 1850
By courtesy of Messrs: Roffé & Raphael, The Vigo Art Galleries, London

PLATE 79

9′ × 7′   VICTORIAN CARPET   c. 1850
By courtesy of Messrs: Roffé & Raphael, The Vigo Art Galleries, London

PLATE 80

14′11″ × 11′11″

VICTORIAN CARPET
By courtesy of Messrs: J. Haim & Co., London

c. 1851

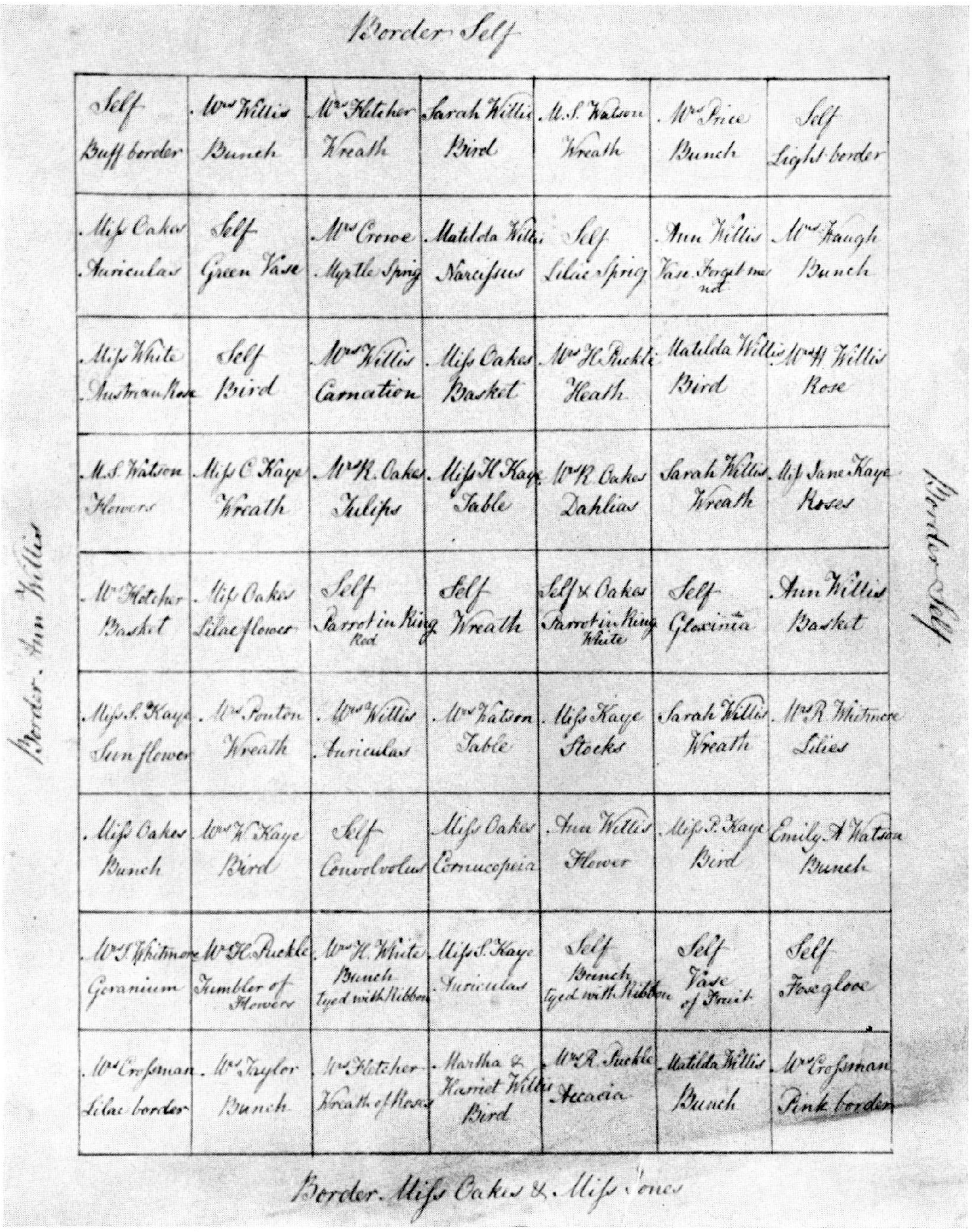

Border Self

Self Buff border	Mrs Willis Bunch	Mrs Fletcher Wreath	Sarah Willis Bird	M.S. Watson Wreath	Mrs Price Bunch	Self Light border
Miss Oakes Auriculas	Self Green Vase	Mrs Crowe Myrtle Sprig	Matilda Willis Narcissus	Self Lilac Sprig	Ann Willis Vase Forget me not	Mrs Haugh Bunch
Miss White Austrian Rose	Self Bird	Mrs Willis Carnation	Miss Oakes Basket	Mrs H. Puckle Heath	Matilda Willis Bird	Mrs H Willis Rose
M.S. Watson Flowers	Miss C Kaye Wreath	Mrs R. Oakes Tulips	Miss H Kaye Table	Mrs R Oakes Dahlias	Sarah Willis Wreath	Miss Jane Kaye Roses
Mrs Fletcher Basket	Miss Oakes Lilac flower	Self Parrot in Ring Red	Self Wreath	Self & Oakes Parrot in Ring White	Self Gloxinia	Ann Willis Basket
Miss S. Kaye Sun flower	Mrs Ponton Wreath	Mrs Willis Auriculas	Mrs Watson Table	Miss Kaye Stocks	Sarah Willis Wreath	Mrs R. Whitmore Lilies
Miss Oakes Bunch	Mrs W. Kaye Bird	Self Convolvolus	Miss Oakes Cornucopia	Ann Willis Flower	Miss P. Kaye Bird	Emily A Watson Bunch
Mrs T. Whitmore Geranium	Mrs H. Puckle Tumbler of Flowers	Mrs H. White Bunch tyed with Ribbon	Miss S. Kaye Auriculas	Self Bunch tyed with Ribbon	Self Vase of Fruit	Self Foxglove
Mrs Crossman Lilac border	Mrs Taylor Bunch	Mrs Fletcher Wreath of Roses	Martha & Harriet Willis Bird	Mrs R. Puckle Acacia	Matilda Willis Bunch	Mrs Crossman Pink border

Border. Ann Willis

Border Self

Border. Miss Oakes & Miss Jones

Plan of the carpet on Plate 80

PLATE 82

VICTORIAN CARPET
By courtesy of V. H. Jinishian, New York

PLATE 83

12′ × 12′   AN EARLY VICTORIAN TILE CARPET   c. 1855
By courtesy of Lord Ogilvy

PLATE 84

15' × 13'3"

VICTORIAN CARPET
By courtesy of Messrs: J. Haim & Co., London

c. 1855

PLATE 85

14′ × 8′6″   VICTORIAN CARPET   c. 1855
By courtesy of Messrs: Roffé & Raphael, The Vigo Art Galleries, London

PLATE 86

7'9" × 5'8" VICTORIAN CARPET c. 1855
By courtesy of Mrs. Lytle Hull, Rhinebeck-on-Hudson, N.Y.

PLATE 87

9'10" × 7'9"   VICTORIAN CARPET   c. 1860
By courtesy of Mrs. William Russell Grace, Aiken, S.C., U.S.A.

PLATE 88

5'9" × 2'8"   VICTORIAN RUG   c. 1860
By courtesy of Messrs: Mayorcas Ltd, London

PLATE 89

12′ × 8′2″   VICTORIAN CARPET   c. 1860
By courtesy of The Victoria and Albert Museum

PLATE 90

9'4" × 7'6" *approx.*

VICTORIAN CARPET

c. 1860

By courtesy of Miss Doris Duke, Calif., U.S.A.

PLATE 91

7′5″ × 5′1″   VICTORIAN RUG   d. 1860
By courtesy of Mrs. Stephen C. Clark Jr., Middleburg, Va.,

PLATE 92

7′6″ × 5′9″

VICTORIAN RUG

c. 1865

By courtesy of Mrs. Stephen C. Clark Jr., Middleburg, Va.,

PLATE 93

13′2″ × 9′   VICTORIAN CARPET   c. 1880
By courtesy of The Tryon Palace, New Bern, N.C., U.S.A.

PLATE 94

7′6″ × 5′ approx.　　　　LATE VICTORIAN RUG　　　　c. 1890
By courtesy of Messrs: J. Haim & Co., London